Spring Security 3.x Cookbook

Over 60 recipes to help you successfully safeguard your web applications with Spring Security

Anjana Mankale

[PACKT] open source*
PUBLISHING   community experience distilled

BIRMINGHAM - MUMBAI

Spring Security 3.x Cookbook

First published: November 2013

Production Reference: 1171113

Published by Packt Publishing Ltd
Livery Place
35 Livery Street
Birmingham B3 2PB, UK

ISBN 978-1-78216-752-5

www.packtpub.com

Cover Image by Aniket Sawant (aniket_sawant_photography@hotmail.com)

Credits

Author

Anjana Mankale

Reviewers

Laurent Frisée

Michael Waluk

Acquisition Editor

Kevin Colaco

Lead Technical Editor

Balaji Naidu

Technical Editors

Aman Preet Singh

Chandni Maishery

Shali Sasidharan

Tarunveer Shetty

Project Coordinator

Wendell Palmar

Proofreader

Bernadette Watkins

Indexer

Priya Subramani

Graphics

Ronak Dhruv

Production Coordinator

Aparna Bhagat

Cover Work

Aparna Bhagat

About the Author

Anjana Mankale is a Tech Lead with 7 years of experience in developing web applications.

She has developed applications for healthcare, e-commerce portals, media portals, and content management systems using Spring and Struts 2. She is extensively involved in application design and implementation. She has worked on Amazon cloud and Spring web services and has recently been involved in deploying and designing a cloud-based multitenant application.

Anjana is passionate about blogging (`http://jtechspace.blogspot.in/`) where she shares her write-ups and technical code that she has worked on.

I would like thank Mr. Dharanidhara Mishra who is a Senior Solution Architect and has been guiding me on application security.

I would also like to thank my husband, Raghavendra S., for his complete support and encouragement by intimating on the timelines.

Lastly I would like to thank my parents and in-laws for their encouragement in completing this book.

About the Reviewers

Laurent Frisée is a freelance consultant with 13 years of experience working for well known as well as less well known companies. He has been a Java developer for the last 10 years and has been involved in the architecture development of the software most of this time. In recent years, he has focused on Java persistence-related problems and is looking forward to working with new technologies (like GWT) or enterprise solutions (like ESB).

Michael Waluk has over 20 years of experience developing secure, scalable software-as-a-service web applications. He has leveraged Spring Security since it was open-sourced as *Acegi Security* in 2004, securing both large and small enterprise projects with it and extending most of its features. Today, millions of people are using these applications to do business securely.

www.PacktPub.com

Support files, eBooks, discount offers and more

You might want to visit www.PacktPub.com for support files and downloads related to your book.

Did you know that Packt offers eBook versions of every book published, with PDF and ePub files available? You can upgrade to the eBook version at www.PacktPub.com and as a print book customer, you are entitled to a discount on the eBook copy. Get in touch with us at service@packtpub.com for more details.

At www.PacktPub.com, you can also read a collection of free technical articles, sign up for a range of free newsletters and receive exclusive discounts and offers on Packt books and eBooks.

http://PacktLib.PacktPub.com

Do you need instant solutions to your IT questions? PacktLib is Packt's online digital book library. Here, you can access, read and search across Packt's entire library of books.

Why Subscribe?

- ▶ Fully searchable across every book published by Packt
- ▶ Copy and paste, print and bookmark content
- ▶ On demand and accessible via web browser

Free Access for Packt account holders

If you have an account with Packt at www.PacktPub.com, you can use this to access PacktLib today and view nine entirely free books. Simply use your login credentials for immediate access.

Table of Contents

Preface

Introduction

Spring Security is a security layer that comes with Spring framework. Spring framework is an active open source project which has made further development of the application easier. It provides various layers to handle different scenarios and challenges that we face during the design and implementation life cycle of the project.

The Spring Security layer of Spring framework is very loosely coupled with the Spring framework, hence it can be easily integrated with other applications.

In this book we will be integrating Spring Security with other frameworks and we will also demonstrate it with coded examples.

What this book covers

Chapter 1, Basic Security, covers the basics of security in a J2ee application. It introduces to the reader the various mechanisms of applying security to authenticate and authorize the users to the application. It also explains container management security.

Chapter 2, Spring Security with Struts 2, provides steps to integrate Spring Security in a Struts 2 application. It demonstrates database authentication and LDAP authentication and authorization with other security mechanism offered by Spring framework.

Chapter 3, Spring Security with JSF, explains all the aspects of Spring Security with a JSF application. It shows how to make the JSF application communicate with Spring Security using listeners.

Chapter 4, Spring Security with Grails, demonstrates how the grails application can seamlessly integrate with Spring Security. We have also shown how Spring Security UI offers screens to create users and roles. We have demonstrated the use of Spring Security tags in GSP pages.

Chapter 5, Spring Security with GWT, focuses on the GWT framework. The GWT framework is integrated with GWT and Spring Security can be used to authenticate and authorize users accessing the GWT application.

Chapter 6, Spring Security with Vaadin, puts forward various options for integrating Spring Security with the Vaadin framework. We have created a sample product catalog application to demonstrate Spring Security integration with the Vaadin framework.

Chapter 7, Spring Security with Wicket, demonstrates the integration of the wicket framework with Spring Security. Wicket itself has an authentication and authorization framework inbuilt, but the challenge was to make wicket use an external framework for authentication and authorization.

Chapter 8, Spring Security with ORM and NoSQL DB, explains Hibernate and MongoDB in authentication and authorization using Spring Security API classes.

Chapter 9, Spring Security with Spring Social, introduces Spring Social, which is a framework developed by Spring Source to provide integration to social networking sites. Spring Social intern uses Spring Security to do the authentication and authorization. The chapter demonstrates how Spring Social and Spring Security integrate with each other by demonstrating a Facebook login application.

Chapter 10, Spring Security with WebServices, explains various options to secure RESTFUL and SOAP based webservices.

Chapter 11, More on Spring Security, is a miscellaneous chapter. It explains integrating Spring Security with the Kaptcha API and providing multiple input authentications.

What you need for this book

In order to complete all the recipes in this book you will need an understanding of the following:

- JBOSS server
- Netbeans
- Maven
- Java
- Tomcat
- Open LDAP
- Apache DS
- Eclipse IDE

Who this book is for

This book is for all Spring-based application developers as well as Java web developers who wish to implement robust security mechanisms into web application development using Spring Security.

Readers are assumed to have a working knowledge of Java web application development, a basic understanding of the Spring framework, and some knowledge of the fundamentals of the Spring Security framework architecture.

Working knowledge of other web frameworks such as Grails and so on would be an added advantage to exploit the whole breadth of recipes provided in this book, but this is not mandatory.

Conventions

In this book, you will find a number of styles of text that distinguish between different kinds of information. Here are some examples of these styles, and an explanation of their meaning.

Code words in text are shown as follows: "We can include other contexts through the use of the `include` directive."

A block of code is set as follows:

```
<%@ page contentType="text/html; charset=UTF-8" %>
<%@ page language="java" %>
<html >
  <HEAD>
    <TITLE>PACKT Login Form</TITLE>
    <SCRIPT>
      function submitForm() {
        var frm = document. myform;
        if( frm.j_username.value == "" ) {
          alert("please enter your username, its empty");
          frm.j_username.focus();
          return ;
        }
```

When we wish to draw your attention to a particular part of a code block, the relevant lines or items are set in bold:

```
<%@ page contentType="text/html; charset=UTF-8" %>
<%@ page language="java" %>
<html >
  <HEAD>
    <TITLE>PACKT Login Form</TITLE>
    <SCRIPT>
```

```
function submitForm() {
  var frm = document. myform;
  if( frm.j_username.value == "" ) {
    alert("please enter your username, its empty");
    frm.j_username.focus();
    return ;
  }
}
```

Any command-line input or output is written as follows:

```
[INFO] Parameter: groupId, Value: com.packt
[INFO] Parameter: artifactId, Value: spring-security-wicket
[INFO] Parameter: version, Value: 1.0-SNAPSHOT
```

New terms and **important words** are shown in bold. Words that you see on the screen, in menus or dialog boxes for example, appear in the text like this: "After clicking on **submit** we need to get an authenticated session."

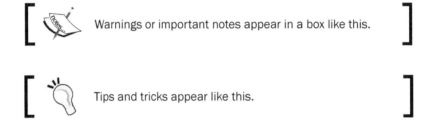

Warnings or important notes appear in a box like this.

Tips and tricks appear like this.

Reader feedback

Feedback from our readers is always welcome. Let us know what you think about this book—what you liked or may have disliked. Reader feedback is important for us to develop titles that you really get the most out of.

To send us general feedback, simply send an e-mail to feedback@packtpub.com, and mention the book title via the subject of your message.

If there is a book that you need and would like to see us publish, please send us a note in the **SUGGEST A TITLE** form on www.packtpub.com or e-mail suggest@packtpub.com. If there is a topic that you have expertise in and you are interested in either writing or contributing to a book, see our author guide on www.packtpub.com/authors.

Customer support

Now that you are the proud owner of a Packt book, we have a number of things to help you to get the most from your purchase.

Downloading the example code

You can download the example code files for all Packt books you have purchased from your account at http://www.PacktPub.com. If you purchased this book elsewhere, you can visit http://www.PacktPub.com/support and register to have the files e-mailed directly to you.

Errata

Although we have taken every care to ensure the accuracy of our content, mistakes do happen. If you find a mistake in one of our books—maybe a mistake in the text or the code—we would be grateful if you would report this to us. By doing so, you can save other readers from frustration and help us improve subsequent versions of this book. If you find any errata, please report them by visiting http://www.packtpub.com/support, selecting your book, clicking on the **errata submission form** link, and entering the details of your errata. Once your errata are verified, your submission will be accepted and the errata will be uploaded on our website, or added to any list of existing errata, under the Errata section of that title. Any existing errata can be viewed by selecting your title from http://www.packtpub.com/support.

Piracy

Piracy of copyright material on the Internet is an ongoing problem across all media. At Packt, we take the protection of our copyright and licenses very seriously. If you come across any illegal copies of our works, in any form, on the Internet, please provide us with the location address or website name immediately so that we can pursue a remedy.

Please contact us at copyright@packtpub.com with a link to the suspected pirated material.

We appreciate your help in protecting our authors, and our ability to bring you valuable content.

Questions

You can contact us at questions@packtpub.com if you are having a problem with any aspect of the book, and we will do our best to address it.

1
Basic Security

In this chapter we will cover:

- ▶ JAAS-based security authentication on JSPs
- ▶ JAAS-based security authentication on servlet
- ▶ Container-based basic authentication on servlet
- ▶ Form-based authentication on servlet
- ▶ Form-based authentication with open LDAP and servlet
- ▶ Hashing/Digest Authentication on servlet
- ▶ Basic authentication for JAX-WS and JAX-RS
- ▶ Enabling and disabling the file listing

Introduction

Authentication and authorization has become a major part of all web applications. Authentication involves checking who is accessing the application. Authorization is a process of checking the access rights of the user. In the native approach, we usually store the user's information in the database and write the code in the application. We also create roles for the user and we do the mapping. Here, it is tightly coupled with the application because we have to rewrite the entire code when we connect to a new database or use any other tools such as LDAP or Kerbose. But there are advance options to handle authentication and authorization. J2EE container provides different ways to authenticate the user by configuring the XML files. We can classify authentication into two types, that is, the container-based authentication and authorization and application level authentication and authorization.

J2EE container provides interfaces and classes to provide authentication. In this chapter, we can see how we authenticate the user using JAAS, basic authentication, and form-based authentication.

In this book, we have used JAAS because it a standard framework for authentication. JAAS works on the **PAM (pluggable authentication module)** framework.

Authentication and authorization can be provided in the following ways:

- Basic authentication: In this technique the application server gives a login form with a username and password textbox, so you don't have to create a login page yourself. You will also know the caller identity.

- Form-based authentication: In this technique the container handles the authentication, but the login form is provided by the user as a JSP page.

- Digest-based authentication: In this method user credentials are hashed with certain algorithms.

- Certificate-based authentication: In this technique the client and the server exchange certificates to verify their identity. Achieving an SSL certificate makes the data transfer over the network secure.

JAAS-based security authentication on JSPs

The deployment descriptor is the main configuration file of all the web applications. The container first looks out for the deployment descriptor before starting any application.

The deployment descriptor is an XML file, `web.xml`, inside the `WEB-INF` folder.

If you look at the XSD of the `web.xml` file, you can see the security-related schema.

The schema can be accessed using the following URL: `http://java.sun.com/xml/ns/j2ee/web-app_2_4.xsd`.

The following is the schema element available in the XSD:

```
<xsd:element name="security-constraint" type="j2ee:security-
  constraintType"/>
<xsd:element name="login-config" type="j2ee:login-configType"/>
<xsd:element name="security-role "type="j2ee:security-roleType"/>
```

Getting ready

You will need the following to demonstrate authentication and authorization:

- JBoss 7
- Eclipse Indigo 3.7
- Create a dynamic web project and name it `Security Demo`
- Create a package, `com.servlets`

▸ Create an XML file in the `WebContent` folder, `jboss-web.xml`

▸ Create two JSP pages, `login.jsp` and `logoff.jsp`

How to do it...

Perform the following steps to achieve JAAS-based security for JSPs:

1. Edit the `login.jsp` file with the input fields `j_username`, `j_password`, and submit it to `SecurityCheckerServlet`:

```
<%@ page contentType="text/html; charset=UTF-8" %>
<%@ page language="java" %>
<html >
  <HEAD>
    <TITLE>PACKT Login Form</TITLE>
    <SCRIPT>
      function submitForm() {
        var frm = document. myform;
        if( frm.j_username.value == "" ) {
          alert("please enter your username, its empty");
          frm.j_username.focus();
          return ;
        }

        if( frm.j_password.value == "" ) {
          alert("please enter the password,its empty");
          frm.j_password.focus();
          return ;
        }
        frm.submit();
      }
    </SCRIPT>
  </HEAD>
  <BODY>
    <FORM name="myform" action="SecurityCheckerServlet"
      METHOD=get>
    <TABLE width="100%" border="0" cellspacing="0" cellpadding=
      "1" bgcolor="white">
    <TABLE width="100%" border="0" cellspacing=
      "0" cellpadding="5">
    <TR align="center">
    <TD align="right" class="Prompt"></TD>
    <TD align="left">
      <INPUT type="text" name="j_username" maxlength=20>
    </TD>
```

```
    </TR>
    <TR align="center">
    <TD align="right" class="Prompt"> </TD>
    <TD align="left">
    <INPUT type="password"
      name="j_password" maxlength=20 >
    <BR>
    <TR align="center">
    <TD align="right" class="Prompt"> </TD>
    <TD align="left">
    <input type="submit" onclick="javascript:submitForm();"
      value="Login">
    </TD>
    </TR>
    </TABLE>
    </FORM>
  </BODY>
</html>
```

The j_username and j_password are the indicators of using form-based
authentication.

2. Let's modify the web.xml file to protect all the files that end with .jsp. If you are
    trying to access any JSP file, you would be given a login form, which in turn calls a
    SecurityCheckerServlet file to authenticate the user. You can also see role
    information is displayed. Update the web.xml file as shown in the following code
    snippet. We have used 2.5 xsd. The following code needs to be placed in between
    the webapp tag in the web.xml file:

```
<display-name>jaas-jboss</display-name>
 <welcome-file-list>
    <welcome-file>index.html</welcome-file>
    <welcome-file>index.htm</welcome-file>
    <welcome-file>index.jsp</welcome-file>
    <welcome-file>default.html</welcome-file>
    <welcome-file>default.htm</welcome-file>
    <welcome-file>default.jsp</welcome-file>
 </welcome-file-list>

 <security-constraint>
    <web-resource-collection>
     <web-resource-name>something</web-resource-name>
     <description>Declarative security tests</description>
     <url-pattern>*.jsp</url-pattern>
```

```
    <http-method>HEAD</http-method>
    <http-method>GET</http-method>
    <http-method>POST</http-method>
    <http-method>PUT</http-method>
    <http-method>DELETE</http-method>
  </web-resource-collection>
  <auth-constraint>
   <role-name>role1</role-name>
  </auth-constraint>
  <user-data-constraint>
   <description>no description</description>
   <transport-guarantee>NONE</transport-guarantee>
  </user-data-constraint>
</security-constraint>
<login-config>
  <auth-method>FORM</auth-method>
  <form-login-config>
   <form-login-page>/login.jsp</form-login-page>
   <form-error-page>/logoff.jsp</form-error-page>
  </form-login-config>
</login-config>
<security-role>
  <description>some role</description>
  <role-name>role1</role-name>
</security-role>
<security-role>
  <description>packt managers</description>
  <role-name>manager</role-name>
</security-role>
<servlet>
  <description></description>
  <display-name>SecurityCheckerServlet</display-name>
  <servlet-name>SecurityCheckerServlet</servlet-name>
  <servlet-class>com.servlets.SecurityCheckerServlet
    </servlet-class>
</servlet>
<servlet-mapping>
  <servlet-name>SecurityCheckerServlet</servlet-name>
  <url-pattern>/SecurityCheckerServlet</url-pattern>
</servlet-mapping>
```

3. JAAS Security Checker and Credential Handler: Servlet is a security checker. Since we are using JAAS, the standard framework for authentication, in order to execute the following program you need to import `org.jboss.security.SimplePrincipal` and `org.jboss.security.auth.callback.SecurityAssociationHandle` and add all the necessary imports. In the following `SecurityCheckerServlet`, we are getting the input from the JSP file and passing it to the `CallbackHandler`.

We are then passing the Handler object to the `LoginContext` class which has the `login()` method to do the authentication. On successful authentication, it will create `Subject` and `Principal` for the user, with user details. We are using iterator interface to iterate the `LoginContext` object to get the user details retrieved for authentication.

In the `SecurityCheckerServlet` Class:

```
package com.servlets;
public class SecurityCheckerServlet extends HttpServlet {
  private static final long serialVersionUID = 1L;

    public SecurityCheckerServlet() {
      super();
    }

    protected void doGet(HttpServletRequest request,
     HttpServletResponse response) throws ServletException,
     IOException {
        char[] password = null;
        PrintWriter out=response.getWriter();
        try
        {

          SecurityAssociationHandler handler = new
            SecurityAssociationHandler();
          SimplePrincipal user = new
            SimplePrincipal(request.getParameter
            ("j_username"));
          password=request.getParameter("j_password").
            toCharArray();
          handler.setSecurityInfo(user, password);
          System.out.println("password"+password);

          CallbackHandler myHandler = new
            UserCredentialHandler(request.getParameter
            ("j_username"),request.getParameter
            ("j_password"));
          LoginContext lc = new LoginContext("other",
            handler);
```

```
        lc.login();

        Subject subject = lc.getSubject();
        Set principals = subject.getPrincipals();

        List l=new ArrayList();
        Iterator it = lc.getSubject().getPrincipals().
          iterator();
        while (it.hasNext()) {
          System.out.println("Authenticated: " +
            it.next().toString() + "<br>");
          out.println("<b><html><body><font
            color='green'>Authenticated: " +
            request.getParameter("j_username")+"
        <br/>"+it.next().toString() +
            "<br/></font></b></body></html>");
            }
        it = lc.getSubject().getPublicCredentials
          (Properties.class).iterator();
        while (it.hasNext())
          System.out.println(it.next().toString());

        lc.logout();
  }       catch (Exception e) {
        out.println("<b><font color='red'>failed
          authenticatation.</font>-</b>"+e);

      }
    }
  protected void doPost(HttpServletRequest request,
  HttpServletResponse response) throws ServletException,
  IOException {
    }

}
```

Create the `UserCredentialHandler` file:

```
package com.servlets;
class UserCredentialHandler implements CallbackHandler {
  private String user, pass;

  UserCredentialHandler(String user, String pass) {
    super();
    this.user = user;
    this.pass = pass;
```

```
    }
    @Override
    public void handle(Callback[] callbacks) throws
      IOException, UnsupportedCallbackException {
        for (int i = 0; i < callbacks.length; i++) {
          if (callbacks[i] instanceof NameCallback) {
            NameCallback nc = (NameCallback) callbacks[i];
            nc.setName(user);
          } else if (callbacks[i] instanceof
              PasswordCallback) {
            PasswordCallback pc = (PasswordCallback)
              callbacks[i];
            pc.setPassword(pass.toCharArray());
          } else {
          throw new UnsupportedCallbackException
            (callbacks[i], "Unrecognized Callback");
        }
      }
    }
  }
}
```

In the `jboss-web.xml` file:

```
<?xml version="1.0" encoding="UTF-8"?>
<jboss-web>
<security-domain>java:/jaas/other</security-domain>
</jboss-web>
```

`Other` is the name of the application policy defined in the `login-config.xml` file.

All these will be packed in as a `.war` file.

4. Configuring the JBoss Application Server. Go to `jboss-5.1.0.GA\server\` `default\conf\login-config.xml` in JBoss. If you look at the file, you can see various configurations for database LDAP and a simple one using the properties file, which I have used in the following code snippet:

```
<application-policy name="other">
  <!-- A simple server login module, which can be used
    when the number of users is relatively small. It uses
    two properties files:
  users.properties, which holds users (key) and their
    password (value).
  roles.properties, which holds users (key) and a comma-
    separated list of
  their roles (value).
  The unauthenticatedIdentity property defines the name of
    the principal
```

```
that will be used when a null username and password are
  presented as is
the case for an unauthenticated web client or MDB. If you
  want to allow such users to be authenticated add the
  property, e.g.,
  unauthenticatedIdentity="nobody"
-->
<authentication>
<login-module
  code="org.jboss.security.auth.spi.UsersRoles
    LoginModule"
  flag="required"/>
  <module-option name="usersProperties">
    users.properties</module-option>
  <module-option name="rolesProperties">
    roles.properties</module-option>
  <module-option name="unauthenticatedIdentity">
    nobody</module-option>
</authentication>
</application-policy>
```

5. Create the `users.properties` file in the same folder. The following is the `Users.`
    `properties` file with username mapped with role.

    User.properties

    ```
    anjana=anjana123
    ```

    roles.properties

    ```
    anjana=role1
    ```

6. Restart the server.

Downloading the example code

You can download the example code files for all Packt books you have
purchased from your account at `http://www.PacktPub.com`. If you
purchased this book elsewhere, you can visit `http://www.PacktPub.`
`com/support` and register to have the files e-mailed directly to you.

How it works...

JAAS consists of a set of interfaces to handle the authentication process. They are:

- The `CallbackHandler` and `Callback` interfaces
- The `LoginModule` interface
- `LoginContext`

The `CallbackHandler` interface gets the user credentials. It processes the credentials and passes them to `LoginModule`, which authenticates the user.

JAAS is container specific. Each container will have its own implementation, here we are using JBoss application server to demonstrate JAAS.

In my previous example, I have explicitly called JASS interfaces.

`UserCredentialHandler` implements the `CallbackHandler` interfaces.

So, `CallbackHandler`s are storage spaces for the user credentials and the `LoginModule` authenticates the user.

`LoginContext` bridges the `CallbackHandler` interface with `LoginModule`. It passes the user credentials to `LoginModule` interfaces for authentication:

```
CallbackHandler myHandler = new UserCredentialHandler(request.
    getParameter("j_username"),request.getParameter("j_password"));
LoginContext lc = new LoginContext("other", handler);
lc.login();
```

The `web.xml` file defines the security mechanisms and also points us to the protected resources in our application.

The following screenshot shows a failed authentication window:

The following screenshot shows a successful authentication window:

See also

- ▸ The *JAAS-based security authentication on servlet* recipe
- ▸ The *Container-based basic authentication on servlet* recipe
- ▸ The *Form-based authentication on servlet* recipe
- ▸ The *Form-based authentication with open LDAP and servlet* recipe
- ▸ The *Hashing/Digest Authentication on servlet* recipe
- ▸ The *Basic authentication for JAX-WS and JAX-RS* recipe
- ▸ The *Enabling and disabling the file listing* recipe

JAAS-based security authentication on servlet

The JAAS-based security authentication on servlet is an extension of JAAS-based security authentication for JSPs. In this section, we are demonstrating that we can even apply security on servlets.

Getting ready

- ▸ Create a new **Web Project** in Eclipse
- ▸ Create a package, `com.packt.security.servlets`
- ▸ Create a Servlet with name `ProtectedServlets`

How to do it...

The following are the steps for JAAS-based security for servlet:

1. Create a servlet and name it `ProtectedServlets`:

```java
public class ProtectedServlets extends HttpServlet {
  private static final long serialVersionUID = 1L;

  public ProtectedServlets() {
    super();

  }
  protected void doGet(HttpServletRequest request,
    HttpServletResponse response) throws ServletException,
    IOException {
    PrintWriter out=response.getWriter();
    try
    {
      out.println("Hello User");
      out.println("Authtype:"+request.getAuthType());
      out.println("User Principal:"+
        request.getUserPrincipal());
      out.println("User role:"+
        request.isUserInRole("role1"));
    }
    catch (Exception e) {
      out.println("<b><font color='red'>failed
        authenticatation</font>-</b>"+e);

    }
  }

  protected void doPost(HttpServletRequest request,
    HttpServletResponse response) throws ServletException,
    IOException {
    // TODO Auto-generated method stub
  }

}
```

2. Now, edit the `web.xml` file to secure the servlet:

```xml
<web-resource-collection>
<web-resource-name>Servlet Protection</web-resource-name>
<description>Declarative security tests</description>
```

```
<url-pattern>/ProtectedServlets</url-pattern>
<http-method>HEAD</http-method>
<http-method>GET</http-method>
<http-method>POST</http-method>
<http-method>PUT</http-method>
<http-method>DELETE</http-method>
</web-resource-collection>
```

How it works...

Restart the server and access the URL: `http://localhost:8080/jaas-jboss/ProtectedServlets`.

You would get a login form, which will authenticate the user. The servlet is the protected resource, and anyone accessing the servlet will be asked to log in. The authentication is handled by JAAS API, which is application-server-specific. Each application server will have its own implementation of security.

See also

- The *Container-based basic authentication on servlet* recipe
- The *Form-based authentication on servlet* recipe
- The *Form-based authentication with open LDAP and servlet* recipe
- The *Hashing/Digest Authentication on servlet* recipe
- The *Basic authentication for JAX-WS and JAX-RS* recipe
- The *Enabling and disabling the file listing* recipe

Container-based basic authentication on servlet

In our previous examples we used interfaces provided by JAAS to authenticate with `loginform.jsp`. The previous application had a custom login form design with authentication handled by JAAS API provided by the application server.

Getting ready

- Create a simple web-app project
- Create a servlet class
- Edit the `web.xml` file for basic authentication
- Add a constraint to restrict the user from accessing the servlet

How to do it...

Now, we will see the basic authentication. The container provides the login form and authenticates the user and redirects the user to the servlet after authentication is successful. There is no login form involved.

Make the following changes in the `web.xml` file:

```
<login-config>
    <auth-method>BASIC</auth-method>
<form-login-config>
```

Export the `.war` to JBoss, restart the server, and access the servlet.

How it works...

In the previous example the container decides the mechanism for authenticating the servlet by reading the `web.xml` file. Here the `<auth-method>` tag has defined `BASIC` as the mode of authentication. We should get a login dialog box popped up when we access the secured resource.

The following screenshots show the workflow of the implementation:

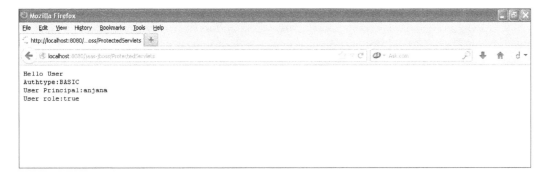

See also

> ▸ The *Form-based authentication on servlet* recipe
>
> ▸ The *Form-based authentication with open LDAP and servlet* recipe
>
> ▸ The *Hashing/Digest Authentication on servlet* recipe
>
> ▸ The *Basic authentication for JAX-WS and JAX-RS* recipe
>
> ▸ The *Enabling and disabling the file listing* recipe

Form-based authentication on servlet

In the previous sections, we demonstrated the basic authentication on servlets and JSPs. Now let's use form-based authentication on servlets.

Getting ready

Let's apply form-based authentication on servlet. You will need a simple web application with a servlet, a web container to handle the authentication, and the web.xml file that tells the container what to authenticate.

How to do it...

Let's see some simple steps for implementing form-based authentication on servlets:

1. Create a JSP file named Containerform.jsp:

```
<%@ page language="java" contentType="text/html;
  charset=ISO-8859-1"
    pageEncoding="ISO-8859-1"%>
<!DOCTYPE html PUBLIC "-//W3C//DTD HTML 4.01 Transitional//EN"
"http://www.w3.org/TR/html4/loose.dtd">
<html>
```

```
<head>
<meta http-equiv="Content-Type" content="text/html;
charset=ISO-8859-1">
<title>Insert title here</title>
</head>
<body>
<form method="POST" action="j_security_check">
Username:<input type="text" name="j_username">
password:<input type="password" name="j_password">
<input type=submit>
</form>
</body>
</html>
```

What do you observe in the previous code?

`action=j_security_check` is the default URL, which is recognized by the web container. It tells the container that it has the user credentials to be authenticated.

2. Now, edit the `web.xml` file:

```
<login-config>
  <auth-method>FORM</auth-method>
  <form-login-config>
    <form-login-page>/Containerform.jsp</form-login-page>
    <form-error-page>/logoff.jsp</form-error-page>
  </form-login-config>
</login-config>
```

Build the project and export the `.war` files to JBoss.

How it works...

The previous example demonstrated the Form-based authentication. The J2EE container reads the `web.xml` file, the `<auth-method>` tag has the `form` attribute set. Then it further looks for the `login.jsp` file, which needs to be displayed to do form-based authentication. The `<form-error-page>` and `<form-login-page>` has the login file name and the error page that needs to be displayed on authentication failure. When the user tries to access the secured resource, the J2EE container redirects the request to the login page. The user credentials are submitted to `j_security_check` action. This action is identified by the container and does the authentication and authorization; on success the user is redirected to the secured resource and on failure the error page shows up.

The following are the screenshots of the workflow which shows the login page for the user and displays the user information on successful authentication:

See also

▸ The *Form-based authentication with open LDAP and servlet* recipe

▸ The *Hashing/Digest Authentication on servlet* recipe

▸ The *Basic authentication for JAX-WS and JAX-RS* recipe

▸ The *Enabling and disabling the file listing* recipe

Form-based authentication with open LDAP and servlet

In this section we will see how we can authenticate users by retrieving the user information stored in open LDAP and JAAS. Open LDAP, as its name suggests, is a free version of the lightweight user directory protocol, which allows us to create groups and add users to it.

Getting ready

Download open LDAP, create roles, groups, and user.

In the JBoss application server, edit the `login-config.xml` file.

How to do it...

Perform the following steps to configure the application server to retrieve users from Open LDAP:

1. In the `login-config.xml` file provide the LDAP port with the URL, credentials, and the domain that needs to be searched to find the username and password provided by the application:

```
<application-policy name="example">
 <authentication>
 <login-module code="org.jboss.security.auth.
  spi.LdapExtLoginModule" flag="required" >
 <module-option name="java.naming.factory.initial">
  com.sun.jndi.ldap.LdapCtxFactory</module-option>
 <module-option name="java.naming.provider.url">
  ldap://localhost:389</module-option>
 <module-option name="java.naming.security.
  authentication">simple</module-option>
 <module-option name="bindDN">cn=Manager,dc=maxcrc,dc=com
  </module-option>
 <module-option name="bindCredential">secret</module-option>
 <module-option name="baseCtxDN">ou=People,
  dc=maxcrc,dc=com</module-option>
 <module-option name="baseFilter">(uid={0})</module-option>

 <module-option name="rolesCtxDN">ou=Roles,
  dc=maxcrc,dc=com</module-option>
  <module-option name="rolesCtxDN">ou=Department,
  dc=maxcrc,dc=com</module-option>
 <module-option name="roleFilter">(member={1})</module-
  option>
 <module-option name="roleAttributeID">cn</module-option>
 <module-option name="searchScope">ONELEVEL_SCOPE</module-
  option>
 <module-option name="allowEmptyPasswords">true</module-
  option>
 </login-module>
 </authentication>
 </application-policy>
```

2. In the `jboss-web.xml` file, we will specify the lookup name for JAAS:

    ```xml
    jboss-web.xml
    <?xml version="1.0" encoding="UTF-8"?>
    <jboss-web>
    <security-domain>java:/jaas/example</security-domain>
    </jboss-web>
    ```

How it works...

Build and deploy the WAR on JBoss, restart the server, and access the browser.

You will be prompted with a login form and JBoss authenticates the user based on the open LDAP credentials provided. The user is retrieved and is authorized with roles mentioned in the application policy. The container provides built-in APIs for authentication. The module `org.jboss.security.auth.spi.LdapExtLoginModule` handles the LDAP authentication process.

See also

- The *Hashing/Digest Authentication on servlet* recipe
- The *Basic authentication for JAX-WS and JAX-RS* recipe
- The *Enabling and disabling the file listing* recipe

Hashing/Digest authentication on servlet

In the previous authentication mechanisms, the client sends the user credentials and the container validates.

The client doesn't attempt to encrypt the password.

So, our application is still not safe and is vulnerable to attacks.

This section is about passing an encrypted user credential to the server and telling the server which encryption algorithm can be used to decrypt the data.

JBoss is the application server that I have chosen to demonstrate it.

Getting ready

- Modify `Login-config.xml`
- Create `encrypt-users. properties`
- Create `encrypt-roles. properties`

How to do it....

1. Modify the `web.xml` file:

```
<login-config>
    <auth-method>DIGEST</auth-method>
    <realm-name>PACKTSecurity</realm-name>
</login-config>
```

2. Now, modify the `jboss-web.xml` file. The realm name is used for hashing:

```
<?xml version="1.0" encoding="UTF-8"?>
<!-- <jboss-web> -->
<!-- <security-domain>java:/jaas/other</security-domain> -->
<!-- </jboss-web> -->
<jboss-web>
<security-domain>java:/jaas/encryptme</security-domain>
</jboss-web>
```

3. Modify the `login-config.xml` file

```
<application-policy name="encryptme">
    <!--this is used to demonstrate DIGEST Authentication
    -->
    <authentication>
      <login-module code="org.jboss.security.auth.
        spi.UsersRolesLoginModule"
        flag="required"/>
    <module-option name="usersProperties">encrypt-
      users.properties</module-option>
    <module-option name="rolesProperties">encrypt-
      roles.properties</module-option>
    <module-option name="hashAlgorithm">MD5</module-option>
    <module-option name="hashEncoding">rfc2617</module-
      option>
    <module-option name="hashUserPassword">false</module-
      option>
    <module-option name="hashStorePassword">true</module-
      option>
    <module-option name="passwordIsA1Hash">true</module-
      option>
    <module-option name="storeDigestCallback">
                org.jboss.security.auth.spi.RFC2617Digest
    </module-option>
    </authentication>
  </application-policy>
```

4. Now, we need to tell JBoss to encrypt the user's password. To do that perform the following steps:

   ❑ Go to `E:\JBOSS5.1\jboss-5.1.0.GA\common\lib`

   ❑ Open `jbosssx-server.jar`

   ❑ Go to the folder where JBoss is installed. I have installed JBoss on my `E:`

   ❑ Now on the command line, write `cd E:\JBOSS5.1\jboss-5.1.0.GA>`

   ❑ And then paste the following command: `java -cp client/jboss-logging-spi.jar;common/lib/jbosssx-server.jar org.jboss.security.auth.spi.RFC2617Digest anjana "PACKTSecurity" role1`

```
C:\WINDOWS\system32\cmd.exe                                           _ □ x
    -disableassertions[:<packagename>...:<classname>]
                 disable assertions with specified granularity
    -esa | -enablesystemassertions
                 enable system assertions
    -dsa | -disablesystemassertions
                 disable system assertions
    -agentlib:<libname>[=<options>]
                 load native agent library <libname>, e.g. -agentlib:hprof
                 see also, -agentlib:jdwp=help and -agentlib:hprof=help
    -agentpath:<pathname>[=<options>]
                 load native agent library by full pathname
    -javaagent:<jarpath>[=<options>]
                 load Java programming language agent, see java.lang.instrument

    -splash:<imagepath>
                 show splash screen with specified image
See http://www.oracle.com/technetwork/java/javase/documentation/index.html for m
ore details.
E:\JBOSS5.1\jboss-5.1.0.GA>java -cp client/jboss-logging-spi.jar;common/lib/jbos
ssx-server.jar org.jboss.security.auth.spi.RFC2617Digest anjana "PACKTSecurity"
anjana123
RFC2617 A1 hash: e3b6b01ec4b0bdd3fc1ff24d0ccabf1f
E:\JBOSS5.1\jboss-5.1.0.GA>
```

   ❑ Now edit `Encrypt-users. properties`:

   `anjana=e3b6b01ec4b0bdd3fc1ff24d0ccabf1f`

   ❑ Encrypt roles and update `roles.properties`

How it works...

The previous example demonstrates the digest authentication mechanism. The password given in the J2EE container is encrypted using the MD5 algorithm. The container decrypts it and verifies the user credentials against the decrypted password. The authentication mechanism is `digest` and the container pops up a login dialog box for the digest mechanism similar to the basic authentication mechanism.

The following screenshot shows the workflow:

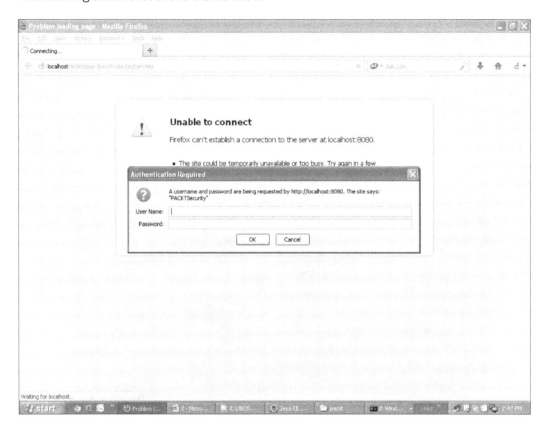

It behaves like basic authentication, but uses the encrypted password along with the realm name to decrypt.

See also

  ▸ The *Basic authentication for JAX-WS and JAX-RS* recipe
  ▸ The *Enabling and disabling the file listing* recipe

Basic authentication for JAX-WS and JAX-RS

The authentication configuration remains the same for JAX-WS and JAX-RS.

We need to give the JAX-WS or JAX-RS URL in `<web-resource collection>`.

`Auth_type` can be basic. The container would come with a form for the user to enter the username and password.

Authentication handled by container

We will first create a web service and then make the container handle the security on it.

Let's create an interface which will expose the `service` method and then declare an `implementation` class.

Let's use Tomcat 6.0 to demonstrate this.

Getting ready

- In Eclipse-Indigo, create a dynamic web project
- Server: Tomcat 6
- JARs to be added to Tomcat `lib` folder: `https://jax-ws.java.net/2.2.7/`
- Download the project and copy the `lib` folder

How to do it...

1. Create an `interface` and an `implementation` class. Add the `@WebService` annotations to it. Create a package named `com.packt.ws`. Create an interface named `EmployeeProfile` and an `implementation` Class:

    Interface:

    ```
    package com.packt.ws;
    import javax.jws.WebMethod;
    import javax.jws.WebService;
    import javax.jws.soap.SOAPBinding;
    import javax.jws.soap.SOAPBinding.Style;
    @WebService
    @SOAPBinding(style = Style.RPC)
    public interface EmployeeProfile {
      @WebMethod
      String getSalary();
    }
    ```

    Implementation:

    ```
    package com.packt.ws;
    import javax.jws.WebService;
    import javax.jws.WebMethod;
    import javax.jws.WebService;
    @WebService(endpointInterface = "com.packt.ws.EmployeeProfile")
    public class EmployeeProfileImpl implements EmployeeProfile {
            @Override
    public String getSalary() {
    ```

```
        return "no salary for the month";
    }
}
```

2. Also add the `sun-jaxws.xml` file under `WEB-INF`

```xml
<?xml version="1.0" encoding="UTF-8"?>
<endpoints
    xmlns="http://java.sun.com/xml/ns/jax-ws/ri/runtime"
    version="2.0">
    <endpoint
        name="EmployeeProfile"
        implementation="com.packt.EmployeeProfileImpl"
        url-pattern="/employee"/>
</endpoints>
```

3. Modify the `web.xml` file as shown:

```xml
<?xml version="1.0" encoding="UTF-8"?>
<web-app xmlns:xsi="http://www.w3.org/2001/XMLSchema-
instance" xmlns="http://java.sun.com/xml/ns/javaee"
xmlns:web="http://java.sun.com/xml/ns/javaee/web-
app_2_5.xsd"
xsi:schemaLocation="http://java.sun.com/xml/ns/javaee
http://java.sun.com/xml/ns/javaee/web-app_2_5.xsd"
id="WebApp_ID" version="2.5">
  <display-name>JAX-WS-Authentication-Tomcat</display-name>
    <listener>
        <listener-class>
            com.sun.xml.ws.transport.http.servlet.
WSServletContextListener
        </listener-class>
    </listener>
    <servlet>
        <servlet-name>employee</servlet-name>
        <servlet-class>
        com.sun.xml.ws.transport.http.servlet.WSServlet
        </servlet-class>
        <load-on-startup>1</load-on-startup>
    </servlet>
    <servlet-mapping>
        <servlet-name>employee</servlet-name>
        <url-pattern>/employee</url-pattern>
    </servlet-mapping>
    <security-role>
      <description>Normal operator user</description>
      <role-name>operator</role-name>
```

```
        </security-role>

<security-constraint>
      <web-resource-collection>
        <web-resource-name>Operator Roles Security</web-
resource-name>
        <url-pattern>/employee</url-pattern>
      </web-resource-collection>

      <auth-constraint>
        <role-name>operator</role-name>
      </auth-constraint>
      <user-data-constraint>
          <transport-guarantee>NONE</transport-guarantee>
      </user-data-constraint>
  </security-constraint>

<login-config>
      <auth-method>BASIC</auth-method>
  </login-config>

</web-app>
```

4. Authenticate the web services. Edit the `tomcat-users.xml` file and add this to `server.xml`:

```
<Realm className="org.apache.catalina.realm.UserDatabaseRealm"
           resourceName="UserDatabase"/>
```

How it works...

By accessing the following URL, you should be prompted for a login.

Each web service URL is authenticated.

You will be prompted with a login page (`http://localhost:8080/EmployeeProfile/employee`)

See also

▸ The *Enabling and disabling the file listing* recipe

Enabling and disabling the file listing

It's generally not advisable to enable directory listing in your application. By default directory listing will be disabled on JBoss.

If it is enabled, go to your JBoss installation folder.

How to do it...

The following steps will help to disable and enable file listing in the application server:

1. Browse to the path `\server\default\deployers\jbossweb.deployer`.

2. Open `web.xml` in the `WEB-INF` folder.

3. Set the listing to `false`.

```
<servlet>
        <servlet-name>default</servlet-name>
        <servlet-class>org.apache.catalina.servlets.DefaultServlet</
servlet-class>
        <init-param>
            <param-name>debug</param-name>
            <param-value>0</param-value>
        </init-param>
        <init-param>
            <param-name>listings</param-name>
            <param-value>false</param-value>
        </init-param>
        <load-on-startup>1</load-on-startup>
    </servlet>
```

See also

▸ The *Spring Security with Struts2* recipe

2
Spring Security with Struts 2

In this chapter we will cover:

- ▶ Integrating Struts 2 with Spring Security
- ▶ Struts 2 application with basic Spring Security
- ▶ Using Struts 2 with digest/hashing-based Spring Security
- ▶ Using Spring Security logout with Struts 2
- ▶ Authenticating databases with Struts 2 and Spring Security
- ▶ Getting the logged-in user info in Struts 2 with Spring Security
- ▶ Displaying custom error messages in Struts 2 for authentication failure
- ▶ Authenticating with ApacheDS with Spring Security and Struts 2 application

Introduction

We learned the basics of security in *Chapter 1, Basic Security*, which helped us to understand Spring Security better and also the origin of the Spring Security component in the Spring Framework.

In this chapter, let's see how Spring Security can be used to authenticate users in a Struts 2 framework-based web application.

Apache Struts 2 can be integrated with JSF and Spring. It is a very flexible POJO Action-based MVC framework. POJO itself performs the role of an action class to fulfill the requests. Struts 2 is derived from another framework called WebWork and it works with servlet filters, which intercept the request and response.

Exploring the Spring package

You can download the JARs from MAVEN directly or add the dependency in your POM file.

We prefer to use the latest JARs 3.1.4 from `http://mvnrepository.com/artifact/`
`org.springframework.security/spring-security-core/`:

```
<dependency>
    <groupId>org.springframework.security</groupId>
    <artifactId>spring-security-core</artifactId>
    <version>3.1.4.RELEASE</version>
 </dependency>
 <dependency>
    <groupId>org.springframework.security</groupId>
    <artifactId>spring-security-web</artifactId>
    <version>3.1.4.RELEASE</version>
  </dependency>
  <dependency>
    <groupId>org.springframework.security</groupId>
    <artifactId>spring-security-config</artifactId>
    <version>3.1.4.RELEASE</version>
  </dependency>
```

Main packages in Spring Security

- `org.springframework.security.authentication`: This is our area of interest
- `org.springframework.security.crypto`: This is used for encryption and decryption
- `org.springframework.security.util`: This is a general utility class used by the Spring Security API
- `org.springframework.security.core`: This contains security core classes related to authentication and authorizations
- `org.springframework.security.access`: This contains voter-based security access control annotations and decision making interfaces
- `org.springframework.security.provisioning`: This contains user and group provisioning interfaces

Key Spring Security features

- Supports JAAS.
- Supports database.
- Supports MongoDB authentication.
- Provides authentication with OpenID.

- Demonstrates multitenancy.
- Provides basic authentication.
- Provides digest authentication.
- Spring Security works like an independent module. Authentication code is handled independently by the Spring Security framework.
- Supports authentication with ApacheDS.
- Supports authentication with Open LDAP.

Authentication mechanism

1. User submits their credentials to the system; that is, a username and password.
2. `org.springframework.security.authentication.` `UsernamePasswordAuthenticationToken` accepts the credentials and passes them to `org.springframework.security.authentication.` `AuthenticationManager` for validation.
3. System authenticates the user.
4. Credential flows as follows: `UsernamePasswordAuthenticationToken` | `AuthenticationManager` | `Authentication`.
5. Finally a fully loaded authentication instance is returned.
6. `SecurityContextHolder` accepts the authentication instance.
7. The system also checks for authorization of roles or groups.
8. Finally, the user is allowed to access the system based on his authorization.

Integrating Struts 2 with Spring Security

Let's first set up a Struts 2 application and integrate Spring Security with it.

Getting ready

- Eclipse Indigo or higher version
- JBoss as server
- Struts 2 JARs: 2.1.x
- Spring-core JARs 3.1.4. Release and Spring-Security 3.1.4.Release
- Struts 2 Spring plugin jar

How to do it...

In this section, we will learn how to set up the Struts 2 application with form-based Spring Security:

1. In your Eclipse IDE, create a dynamic web project and name it `Spring_Security_Struts2`.

2. Create a source folder at `src/main/java`.

3. Create a `struts.xml` file under the source folder `src/main/java`.

4. To integrate Struts 2 with the Spring application, add the `application-context.xml` file reference here.

5. Add the Struts filter mapping in `web.xml`. Spring listener also needs to be added to the `web.xml` file. The listener entry should be above the Struts 2 filter entry.

6. The `contextLoaderListener` will tell the `servletcontainer` about the `springcontextLoader` and it will track events. This also allows the developers to create `BeanListeners`, which allow it to track events in the Bean.

7. In the `web.xml` file, add the following code:

```
<?xml version="1.0" encoding="UTF-8"?>
<web-app xmlns:xsi="http://www.w3.org/2001/XMLSchema-
instance" xmlns="http://java.sun.com/xml/ns/javaee"
xmlns:web="http://java.sun.com/xml/ns/javaee/web-app_2_5.xsd"
xsi:schemaLocation=
"http://java.sun.com/xml/ns/javaee
http://java.sun.com/xml/ns/javaee/web-app_2_5.xsd"
id="WebApp_ID" version="2.5">
<display-name>Struts2x</display-name>
<listener>
<listener-class>org.springframework.web.
context.ContextLoaderListener</listener-class>
</listener>
<!—to integrate spring with struts2->
<context-param>
<param-name>contextConfigLocation</param-name>
<param-value>/WEB-INF/applicationContext.xml</param-value>
</context-param>
<filter>
<filter-name>struts2</filter-name>
<filter-class>org.apache.struts2.dispatcher.FilterDispatcher</
filter-class>
</filter>
```

```
<filter-mapping>
<filter-name>struts2</filter-name>
<url-pattern>/*</url-pattern>
</filter-mapping>

</web-app>
```

8. To set up form-based security, we need to create `login.jsp`. The form action is `j_spring_security_check`:

```
<%@ taglib prefix="c" url="http://java.sun.com/jsp/jstl/core"%>
<html>
  <head>
  <title>Login Page</title>
  <style>
    .errorblock {
      color: #ff0000;
      background-color: #ffEEEE;
      border: 3px solid #ff0000;
      padding: 8px;
      margin: 16px;
    }
  </style>
  </head>
  <body onload='document.f.j_username.focus();'>
    <h3>Login with Username and Password (Custom Page)</h3>
    <% String error=request.getParameter("error");

    if(error!=null){
      %>

      <div class="errorblock">
      Your login attempt was not successful, try again.
        <br /> Caused :

      </div>

    <%} %>
    <form name='f' action="<c:url
      value='/j_spring_security_check'/>"
    method='POST'>

    <table>
      <tr>
        <td>User:</td>
        <td><input type='text' name='j_username' value=''>
        </td>
```

```
    </tr>
    <tr>
      <td>Password:</td>
      <td><input type='password' name='j_password' />
      </td>
    </tr>
    <tr>
      <td colspan='2'><input name="submit" type="submit"
      value="submit" />
      </td>
    </tr>
    <tr>
      <td colspan='2'><input name="reset" type="reset" />
      </td>
    </tr>
  </table>

  </form>
 </body>
</html>
```

9. Create a folder and name it `secure/hello.jsp`.

10. Map the `login` action with `login.jsp`.

11. Map the `loginfailed` action with `login.jsp?error=true`.

12. Map the `welcome` action with `secure/hello.jsp` with the action class-`HelloWorld`:

`struts.xml`:

```
<!DOCTYPE struts PUBLIC
"-//Apache Software Foundation//DTD Struts Configuration 2.0//EN"
"http://struts.apache.org/dtds/struts-2.0.dtd">
<struts>
  <package name="default" namespace="/" extends="struts-
    default">
  <action name="helloWorld">
    <result>success.jsp</result>
  </action>

  <action name="login">
    <result>login.jsp</result>
  </action>

  <action name="loginfailed">
    <result>login.jsp?error=true</result>
  </action>
```

```
<action name="welcome" >
  <result>secure/hello.jsp</result>
</action>

</package>
</struts>
```

13. The `login page` URL is mapped with the Struts 2 action `'/login'`.

14. Security is applied on the Struts 2 action `'/welcome'`.

15. The user will be prompted to login.

16. The user with `role_user` will be authorized to access the pages

`Applicationcontext-security.xml:`

```
<beans:beans xmlns="http://www.springframework.org
/schema/security"
   xmlns:beans="http://www.springframework.org
/schema/beans"
   xmlns:xsi="http://www.w3.org/2001/XMLSchema-instance"
   xsi:schemaLocation="http://www.springframework.org
/schema/beans
   http://www.springframework.org/schema/beans/spring-
beans-3.0.xsd
   http://www.springframework.org/schema/security
   http://www.springframework.org/schema/security/spring-
security-3.1.xsd">

 <global-method-security pre-post-annotations="enabled">
        <!-- AspectJ pointcut expression that locates our "post"
method and applies security that way
        <protect-pointcut expression="execution(*
bigbank.*Service.post*(..))" access="ROLE_TELLER"/>
        -->
   </global-method-security>
   <http auto-config="true" use-expressions="true" >
        <intercept-url pattern="/welcome"
access="hasRole('ROLE_USER')"/>
        <form-login login-page="/login" default-target-
url="/welcome" authentication-failure-
url="/loginfailed?error=true" />
        <logout/>
   </http>
    <authentication-manager>
     <authentication-provider>
       <user-service>
```

```
        <user name="anjana" password="packt123"
authorities="ROLE_USER" />
        </user-service>
      </authentication-provider>
    </authentication-manager>

</beans:beans>
```

How it works...

Just run the application. You will be provided with a link to access the secured page. On clicking on the link you will be prompted to log in. This is actually a form-based login.

Here on submit, the action is sent to the Spring Framework which authenticates the user.

On success, the user will see the authenticated page.

The Struts 2 framework easily gels with the Spring Framework and its modules with very minor modification.

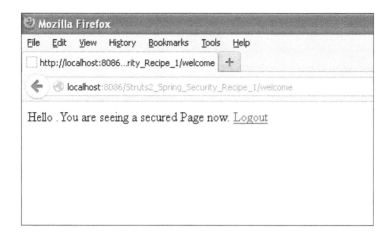

See also

▶ The *Struts 2 application with basic Spring Security* recipe

▶ The *Using Struts 2 with digest/hashing-based Spring Security* recipe

▶ The *Displaying custom error messages in Struts 2 for authentication failure* recipe

▶ The *Authenticating databases with Struts 2 and Spring Security* recipe

▶ The *Authenticating with ApacheDS with Spring Security and Struts 2 application* recipe

▶ The *Using Spring Security logout with Struts 2* recipe

▶ The *Getting the logged-in user info in Struts 2 with Spring Security* recipe

Struts 2 application with basic Spring Security

In this section we will demonstrate basic Spring Security authentication with Struts 2. We will create a sample Struts 2 application and add Spring Security features to the action to make it secured. Only authenticated authorized users can access it.

Getting ready

▶ Update the `Applicationcontext-security.xml` file

▶ Create a new dynamic project in Eclipse: `Struts2_Spring_BASIC_Security_Recipe2`

How to do it...

Perform the following steps for integrating the Struts 2 application with Spring Security to implement basic authentication:

1. Modify the `applicationcontext-security.xml` file to support basic security:

   `Applicationcontext-security.xml:`

   ```xml
   <beans:beans xmlns="http://www.springframework.org
   /schema/security"
      xmlns:beans="http://www.springframework.org
   /schema/beans"
      xmlns:xsi="http://www.w3.org/2001/XMLSchema-instance"
      xsi:schemaLocation="http://www.springframework.org
   /schema/beans
      http://www.springframework.org/schema/beans/spring-
   beans-3.0.xsd
      http://www.springframework.org/schema/security
      http://www.springframework.org/schema/security/spring-security-
   3.1.xsd">

    <global-method-security pre-post-annotations="enabled">
         <!-- AspectJ pointcut expression that locates our "post"
   method and applies security that way
         <protect-pointcut expression="execution(*
   bigbank.*Service.post*(..))" access="ROLE_TELLER"/>
         -->
      </global-method-security>

     <http>
       <intercept-url pattern="/welcome" access="ROLE_TELLER"
   />
       <http-basic />
     </http>
      <authentication-manager>
        <authentication-provider>
          <user-service>
            <user name="anjana" password="123456"
   authorities="ROLE_TELLER" />
          </user-service>
        </authentication-provider>
      </authentication-manager>
   </beans:beans>
   ```

How it works...

When the user runs the Struts 2 application and tries to access the secured resource, the Spring Security context is initialized and the Struts 2 action is interrupted with Spring's login dialog box, which will request the username and password. On successful authentication, the user will be redirected to the Struts 2 action page.

The following is the workflow of the application:

Struts 2 and Spring basic security on browser:

See also

▸ The *Using Struts 2 with digest/hashing-based Spring Security* recipe

Using Struts 2 with digest/hashing-based Spring Security

Using the form-based or basic authentication doesn't make the Struts 2-based application secure since the passwords are exposed to the user as plain text. There is a crypto package available in Spring Security JAR. The package can decrypt the encrypted password, but we need to tell the Spring Security API about the algorithm used for encryption.

Getting ready

▸ Create a dynamic web project in Eclipse

▸ Add the Struts 2 JARs

- ▶ Add Spring Security related JARs
- ▶ The `web.xml`, `struts2.xml`, and JSP settings remain the same as the previous application

How to do it...

Let's encrypt the password: `packt123456`.

We need to use an external JAR, `JACKSUM`, which means Java checksum. It supports both MD5 and SHA1 encryption.

Download the `jacksum.zip` file (`http://www.jonelo.de/java/jacksum/#Download`) and extract the ZIP folder.

```
packt>java -jar jacksum.jar -a sha -q"txt:packt123456"
```

Update the `applicationcontext-security.xml` file:

```
<beans:beans xmlns="http://www.springframework.org
/schema/security"
    xmlns:beans="http://www.springframework.org/schema/beans"
    xmlns:xsi="http://www.w3.org/2001/XMLSchema-instance"
    xsi:schemaLocation="http://www.springframework.org/schema/beans
    http://www.springframework.org/schema/beans/spring-beans-
3.0.xsd
    http://www.springframework.org/schema/security
    http://www.springframework.org/schema/security/spring-security-
3.1.xsd">

  <global-method-security pre-post-annotations="enabled">
        <!-- AspectJ pointcut expression that locates our "post"
method and applies security that way
        <protect-pointcut expression="execution(* bigbank.*Service.
post*(..))" access="ROLE_TELLER"/>
        -->
    </global-method-security>
  <http>
    <intercept-url pattern="/welcome" access="ROLE_TELLER" />
```

```
    <http-basic />
  </http>
  <authentication-manager>
      <authentication-provider>
  <password-encoder hash="sha" />
      <user-service>
          <user name="anjana" password="bde892ed4e131546a2f9997cc94d31
e2c8f18b2a"
              authorities="ROLE_TELLER" />
      </user-service>
  </authentication-provider>
  </authentication-manager>
</beans:beans>
```

How it works...

We need to update the `Applicationcontext-security.xml` file. Observe that the type of authentication is basic but the password is hashed using the algorithm. We want the Spring Security to decrypt it using the SHA algorithm and authenticate the user.

Spring Security is very flexible in handling digest authentication. You can also see that there is no container-based dependency.

Basic authentication from the browser can be seen in the following screenshot:

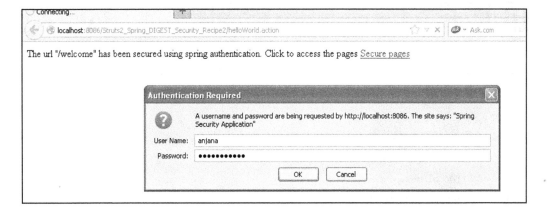

Spring has authenticated the user by decrypting the password:

See also

▸ The *Displaying custom error messages in Struts 2 for authentication failure* recipe

▸ The *Authenticating databases with Struts 2 and Spring Security* recipe

▸ The *Authenticating with ApacheDS with Spring Security and Struts 2 application* recipe

▸ The *Using Spring Security logout with Struts 2* recipe

▸ The *Getting the logged-in user info in Struts 2 with Spring Security* recipe

Using Spring Security logout with Struts 2

In this section let us implement a logout scenario, where the logged-in user will be logged out of the application. The logout action will be handled by the Spring Security framework. We need to configure the `struts.xml` file to handle the `j_spring_security_logout` action.

Getting ready

▸ Create a dynamic web project in Eclipse

▸ Add the Struts 2 related JARs

▸ Add Spring Security-related JARs

▸ The `web.xml`, `struts2.xml`, and JSP settings remain the same as the previous application

How to do it...

1. Let's update the secure page, `hello.jsp`:

```
<%@ taglib prefix="c" uri="http://java.sun.com/jsp/jstl/core"%>
<%@page import="java.security.Principal" %>
<html>
<body>
Hello .You are seeing a secured Page now.

    <a href="<c:url value="/j_spring_security_logout" />" >
Logout</a>
 </body>
</html>
```

2. Let's map the `j_spring_security_logout` with the `struts.xml` file:

   When the user clicks on **logout**, the user will be logged out and will be redirected to `index.jsp`.

```
<!DOCTYPE struts PUBLIC
"-//Apache Software Foundation//DTD Struts Configuration 2.0//EN"
"http://struts.apache.org/dtds/struts-2.0.dtd">
<struts>
    <package name="default" namespace="/" extends="struts-default">
        <action name="helloWorld">
            <result>success.jsp</result>
        </action>

      <action name="login">
                <result>login.jsp</result>
         </action>

         <action name="loginfailed">
                <result>login.jsp?error=true</result>
         </action>

         <action name="welcome" >
         <result>secure/hello.jsp</result>
         </action>

     <action name="j_spring_security_logout">
     <result>index.jsp</result>
         </action>
     </package>
</struts>
```

3. Update the `applicationcontext-security.xml` file:

```xml
<beans:beans xmlns="http://www.springframework.org/schema/
security"
    xmlns:beans="http://www.springframework.org
/schema/beans"
    xmlns:xsi="http://www.w3.org/2001/XMLSchema-instance"
    xsi:schemaLocation="http://www.springframework.org
/schema/beans
    http://www.springframework.org/schema/beans/spring-
beans-3.0.xsd
    http://www.springframework.org/schema/security
    http://www.springframework.org/schema/security/spring-
security-3.1.xsd">

  <global-method-security pre-post-annotations="enabled">
    </global-method-security>
  <http>
    <intercept-url pattern="/welcome" access="ROLE_TELLER"
/>
    <logout logout-success-url="/helloWorld" />
    <http-basic />
  </http>
    <authentication-manager>
      <authentication-provider>
    <password-encoder hash="sha" />
      <user-service>
        <user name="anjana" password="bde892ed4e131546a2f9997cc94
d31e2c8f18b2a"
            authorities="ROLE_TELLER" />
      </user-service>
    </authentication-provider>
    </authentication-manager>
</beans:beans>
```

How it works...

Spring Security also provides options to handle logout. When the user clicks on **logout**, the user is directed to the assigned page.

`j_spring_secuurity_logout` provides the logout option for the Struts 2 application.

The Struts 2 application has the map and the URL with its action.

The logout option is usually given in the secured pages.

There's more...

Till now we have stored the authentication information in the `.xml` file. We have also hashed the password. How about storing the information on the external system and getting it? Let's see how Struts 2 works with this database authentication in the following section.

See also

▶ The *Displaying custom error messages in Struts 2 for authentication failure* recipe

▶ The *Authenticating databases with Struts 2 and Spring Security* recipe

▶ The *Authenticating with ApacheDS with Spring Security and Struts 2 application* recipe

▶ The *Getting the logged-in user info in Struts 2 with Spring Security* recipe

Authenticating databases with Struts 2 and Spring Security

In this section, let us authorize the user who logs into the Struts 2 application using the information stored in the database. Spring Security needs to be configured in Struts 2 application such that it gets to know the location of the database and SQL that needs to be executed to authenticate the user using Spring Security.

Getting ready

▶ Create a dynamic web project in Eclipse: `Struts2_Spring_DBAuthentication_Recipe4`

▶ Copy the `struts.xml` file to `src/main/java`

▶ Add the `db-beans.xml` file to `WEB-INF`

▶ Copy the `webContent` folder from the previous recipe

▶ Add the following JARs into the `lib` folder or update your POM file if you are using maven:

  ❑ spring-jdbc-3.0.7.RELEASE

  ❑ mysql-connector-java-5.1.17

  ❑ commons-dbcp

  ❑ commons-pool-1.5.4

How to do it...

1. To perform database authentication with Struts 2 and Spring, we need to create a db-beans.xml file. The db-beans.xml file will have database information:

```xml
<beans xmlns="http://www.springframework.org/schema/beans"
    xmlns:xsi="http://www.w3.org/2001/XMLSchema-instance"
    xsi:schemaLocation="http://www.springframework.org/schema/beans
    http://www.springframework.org/schema/beans/spring-beans-
3.0.xsd">
    <bean id="MySqlDatasource" class="org.springframework.jdbc.
datasource.DriverManagerDataSource">
    <property name="driverClassName" value="com.mysql.jdbc.Driver"
/>
    <property name="url" value="jdbc:mysql://localhost:3306/test1"
/>
    <property name="username" value="root" />
    <property name="password" value="prdc123" />
    </bean>
</beans>
```

2. Add the db-beans.xml file in the same place as applicationcontext-security.xml. Update the web.xml file to read the db-beans.xml file:

```xml
<?xml version="1.0" encoding="UTF-8"?>
<web-app xmlns:xsi="http://www.w3.org/2001/XMLSchema-instance"
xmlns="http://java.sun.com/xml/ns/javaee" xmlns:web="http://java.
sun.com/xml/ns/javaee/web-app_2_5.xsd" xsi:schemaLocation=
"http://java.sun.com/xml/ns/javaee
http://java.sun.com/xml/ns/javaee/web-app_2_5.xsd"
id="WebApp_ID" version="2.5">
  <display-name>SpringStruts2Security</display-name>
 <context-param>
        <param-name>contextConfigLocation</param-name>
        <param-value>
            /WEB-INF/db-beans.xml,
            /WEB-INF/applicationContext-security.xml
        </param-value>
    </context-param>

  <filter>
    <filter-name>springSecurityFilterChain</filter-name>
    <filter-class>
                org.springframework.web.filter.
DelegatingFilterProxy
                </filter-class>
```

```xml
    </filter>
    <filter-mapping>
      <filter-name>springSecurityFilterChain</filter-name>
      <url-pattern>/*</url-pattern>
    </filter-mapping>
    <filter>
      <filter-name>struts2</filter-name>
      <filter-class>org.apache.struts2.dispatcher.ng.filter.
StrutsPrepareAndExecuteFilter</filter-class>
    </filter>
    <listener>
      <listener-class>org.springframework.web.context.
ContextLoaderListener</listener-class>
    </listener>
    <filter-mapping>
      <filter-name>struts2</filter-name>
      <url-pattern>/*</url-pattern>
    </filter-mapping>
    <error-page>
            <error-code>403</error-code>
            <location>/secure/denied.jsp</location>
     </error-page>

    <welcome-file-list>
      <welcome-file>index.jsp</welcome-file>
    </welcome-file-list>
  </web-app>
```

3. Run the following SQL script in your database:

```sql
CREATE TABLE `users1` (  `USER_ID` INT(10) UNSIGNED NOT NULL,
  `USERNAME` VARCHAR(45) NOT NULL,
  `PASSWORD` VARCHAR(45) NOT NULL,
  `ENABLED` tinyint(1) NOT NULL,
  PRIMARY KEY (`USER_ID`)
) ENGINE=InnoDB DEFAULT CHARSET=utf8;
CREATE TABLE `user_roles` (
  `USER_ROLE_ID` INT(10) UNSIGNED NOT NULL,
  `USER_ID` INT(10) UNSIGNED NOT NULL,
  `ROLE` VARCHAR(45) NOT NULL,
  PRIMARY KEY (`USER_ROLE_ID`),
  KEY `FK_user_roles` (`USER_ID`),
  CONSTRAINT `FK_user_roles` FOREIGN KEY (`USER_ID`) REFERENCES
`users` (`USER_ID`)
) ENGINE=InnoDB DEFAULT CHARSET=utf8;
```

```
INSERT INTO test1.users (USER_ID, USERNAME,PASSWORD, ENABLED)
VALUES (100, 'anjana', 'packt123456', TRUE);

INSERT INTO test1.user_roles (USER_ROLE_ID, USER_ID,AUTHORITY)
VALUES (1, 100, 'ROLE_TELLER');
```

4. Update the `applicationContext-security.xml` file to read the database configuration:

```xml
<beans:beans xmlns="http://www.springframework.org/schema/
security"
   xmlns:beans="http://www.springframework.org
/schema/beans"
   xmlns:xsi="http://www.w3.org/2001/XMLSchema-instance"
   xsi:schemaLocation="http://www.springframework.org
/schema/beans
   http://www.springframework.org/schema/beans/spring-
beans-3.0.xsd
   http://www.springframework.org/schema/security
   http://www.springframework.org/schema/security/spring-
security-3.1.xsd">

 <global-method-security pre-post-annotations="enabled">
       <!-- AspectJ pointcut expression that locates our "post"
method and applies security that way
       <protect-pointcut expression="execution(*
bigbank.*Service.post*(..))" access="ROLE_TELLER"/>
       -->
    </global-method-security>

  <http>
    <intercept-url pattern="/welcome" access="ROLE_TELLER"
/>
    <logout logout-success-url="/helloWorld" />
    <http-basic />
  </http>

  <authentication-manager>
     <authentication-provider>
        <jdbc-user-service data-source-ref="MySqlDS"

            users-by-username-query="
               select username,password, enabled
              from users1 where username=?"

            authorities-by-username-query="
              select u.username, ur.role from users1 u,
user_roles ur
```

```
                where u.user_id = ur.user_id and u.username =?   "
                />
            </authentication-provider>
        </authentication-manager>
    </beans:beans>
```

How it works...

Struts 2 Framework gives a link to access the secured page. But the Spring Security framework interrupts and gives an authentication dialog box .The authentication is done by Spring Security Framework by querying the database. The authentication manager is configured with the datasource ref, which will load information for the security framework to authenticate the user based on the query.

There's more...

So far we applied security with just a JSP file, which is mapped without action in `struts2.xml`. Let's see how we can map an action class with JSP, and then integrate with Spring Security. Ideally it should work in the same way. Let's get the logged-in user information in the action class and display it on the browser.

See also

- ▶ The *Displaying custom error messages in Struts 2 for authentication failure* recipe
- ▶ The *Authenticating with ApacheDS with Spring Security and Struts 2 application* recipe
- ▶ The *Getting the logged-in user info in Struts 2 with Spring Security* recipe

Getting the logged-in user info in Struts 2 with Spring Security

So far in our examples we have not used any Struts 2 action class.

Let's create an action class and see how Security behaves with this action class. We will use form-based authentication with this recipe.

Getting ready

So far in our examples we have not used any Struts 2 action class.

Let's create an action class and see how security behaves with this action class. We will use form-based authentication with this recipe:

▸ Create a dynamic web project: `Struts2_Spring_Security_Recipe5`

▸ Create a package: `com.packt.action`

▸ Copy the `struts.xml` file from the previous recipe in `src/main/java`

▸ Also copy the `WebContent` folder

▸ We need to add an action class to the package

▸ Update the `struts.xml` file

How to do it...

1. The `HelloAction` file is as follows:

```
package com.packt.action;
public class HelloAction {
        public String execute(){
        return "SUCCESS";
    }
}
```

2. Update the `Struts.xml` file with `HelloAction`. So when the user is authenticated, it will pass the request to the action class which will execute the `execute()` method, and then will be redirected to `hello.jsp`:

```
<!DOCTYPE struts PUBLIC
"-//Apache Software Foundation//DTD Struts Configuration 2.0//EN"
"http://struts.apache.org/dtds/struts-2.0.dtd">
<struts>
    <package name="default" namespace="/" extends="struts-default">
        <action name="helloWorld">
            <result>success.jsp</result>
        </action>

    <action name="login">
            <result>login.jsp</result>
        </action>

        <action name="loginfailed">
            <result>login.jsp?error=true</result>
        </action>

        <action name="welcome"
          class="com.packt.action.HelloAction">
```

```
<result name="SUCCESS">secure/hello.jsp</result>
</action>

</package>
</struts>
```

3. Getting the logged in user:

We can get the logged in username in the action class and we can display it on the page or use it further in our application.

We can use `request.getUserPrincipal` in our action class to get the logged in user information.

4. For the project setup:

   ❑ Create a dynamic web project in Eclipse: `Struts2_Spring_Security_Recipe6`

   ❑ Copy the `src/main/java` folder from the previous recipe

   ❑ Copy the `Web content` folder from the previous recipe

   ❑ Modify the `HelloAction.java` file

```java
package com.packt.action;
import javax.servlet.http.HttpServletRequest;
import org.apache.struts2.ServletActionContext;
public class HelloAction {
    private String name;
                public String execute(){
                HttpServletRequest request = ServletActionContext.
getRequest();
                String logged_in_user=request.getUserPrincipal().
getName();
                setName(logged_in_user);
                return "SUCCESS";
        }

        public String getName() {
                return name;
        }

        public void setName(String name) {
                this.name = name;
        }
}
```

❑ Modify the `secure/Hello.jsp` file:

```
<%@ taglib prefix="c" uri="http://java.sun.com/jsp/jstl/core"%>
<%@taglib uri="/struts-tags" prefix="s" %>
<%@page import="java.security.Principal" %>
<html>
  <body>
    Hello <h1><s:property value="name" /></h1>.You are
      seeing a secured Page now.
    <a href="<c:url value="/j_spring_security_logout" />" >
      Logout</a>
  </body>
</html>
```

How it works...

The user information is stored in principal:

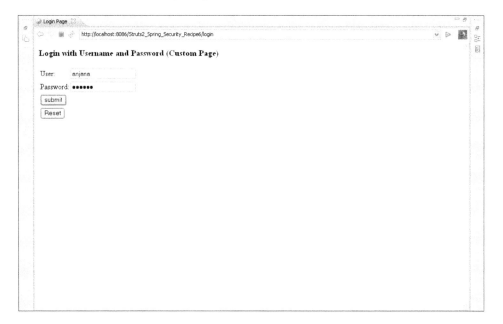

Displaying the logged in user on the browser:

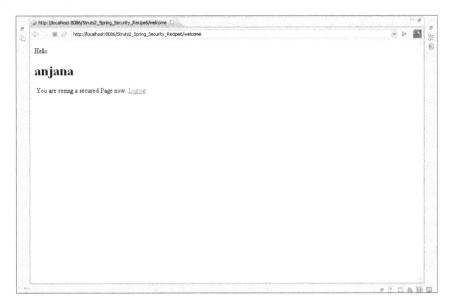

There's more...

After displaying the user information, we can display the custom error message to the user on authentication failure.

See also

- ▶ The *Displaying custom error messages in Struts 2 for authentication failure* recipe
- ▶ The *Authenticating with ApacheDS with Spring Security and Struts 2 application* recipe

Displaying custom error messages in Struts 2 for authentication failure

In this section, we will capture the authentication failure message from Spring Security in our Struts 2 application and see how this can be displayed to the user.

Getting ready

▶ Redirect to failure action on authentication failure

▶ Display a custom message to the user

How to do it...

Perform the following steps for capturing Spring Security's authentication failure messages in the JSP application:

1. In the `applicationcontext.xml` file, we can redirect the URL to another action: `Authentication-failure-url="/loginfailed? error=true"`.

```
<http auto-config="true" use-expressions="true" >
        <intercept-url pattern="/welcome" access="hasRole('ROLE_
TELLER')"/>
        <form-login login-page="/login" default-target-url="/
welcome" authentication-failure-url="/loginfailed?error=true" />
        <logout/>
   </http>
```

2. Update the `login.jsp` page with the following code:

```
<% String error=request.getParameter("error");

 if(error!=null){
 %>

        <div class="errorblock">
              Your login attempt was not successful, try
                again.<br /> Caused :

        </div>

   <%} %>
```

How it works...

Login failed action is mapped with the `login.jsp` file in `struts2.xml`. The `authentication-failure-url` is added in the `application-context.xml`. When the user enters the wrong credentials, authentication fails and the user is redirected to the login page with an error message.

The error message configuration is done in the JSP file.

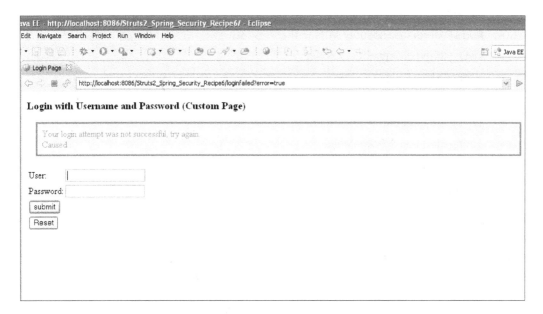

See also

▶ The *Authenticating with ApacheDS with Spring Security and Struts 2 application* recipe

Authenticating with ApacheDS with Spring Security and Struts 2 application

In this section, we will be storing the user credentials and role information in the Apache directory server. Spring Security has to locate the server and log in to the server. It should authenticate the user by comparing the credentials submitted by the user and the credentials and role information present in the Apache directory server.

Getting ready

▶ Create a dynamic web project in Eclipse

▶ The `src/main/java` folder and the `WebContent` Folder remain the same

▶ Install Apache directory studio: 1.5.3

- ▸ Install Apache directory server: 2.0
- ▸ 10389 is the apache-ds port
- ▸ Add LDAP-related security JARs to the `WebContent Lib` folder
- ▸ spring-ldap-core-tiger-1.3.X release
- ▸ spring-ldap-odm-1.3.X release
- ▸ spring-security-ldap-1.3.X release
- ▸ spring-ldap-ldif-batch-1.3.X release
- ▸ spring-ldap-test-1.3.X release
- ▸ spring-ldap-core-1.3.X release
- ▸ spring-ldap-ldif-core-1.3.X release

How to do it...

Perform the following steps to set up Apache directory to authenticate users in the Struts 2 application using Spring Security:

1. Configure the Apache DS Server after installing the mentioned prerequisites.
2. Create a partition using the following steps:
   - ❑ Open the `server.xml` file: `C:\Program Files\Apache Directory Server\instances\default\conf\server.xml`.
   - ❑ Add JDM partition: `<jdbmPartition id="packt" suffix="o=packt"/>`.
   - ❑ You can restart the Apache DS Server to see the changes. Then connect to Apache DS using the Apache Directory Studio. Right Click on **DIT**. Create **Entry** from **Scratch**. Select **Organization**, select **o** and in the **Value** enter `packt`. Select **Finish** and refresh the **DIT** to see the updates.
3. Configure Apache Directory studio.
4. Connect to the Apache directory server.
5. Apache DS runs on 10389.
6. Create two groups `ou=groups` and `ou=user`.

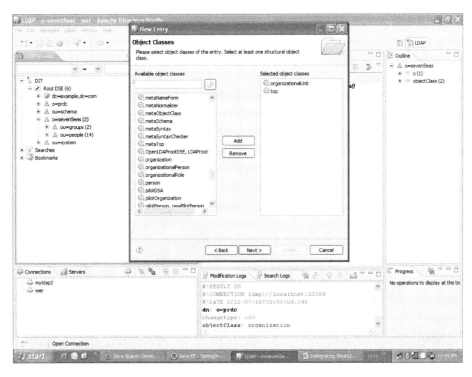

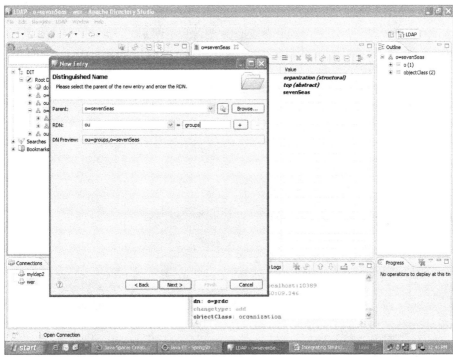

7. Here, object class is for adding entries to `ou=groups`, since this maintains the role:

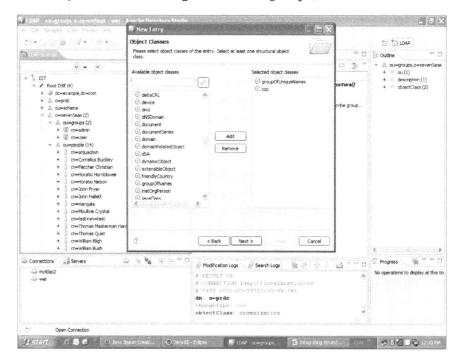

8. Here, object class is to add entries to `ou=people`:

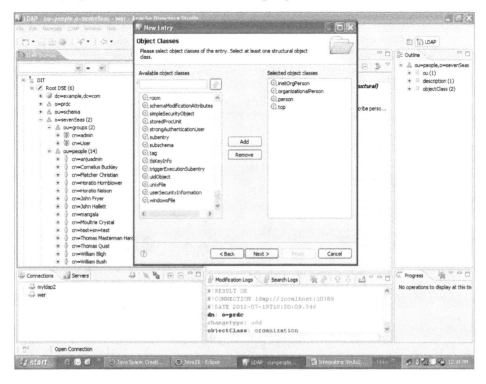

9. Assign roles to users by adding `UniqueMember` to `cn=admin`.

```
Spring-security-ldap.xml:
```

```xml
<beans:beans xmlns="http://www.springframework.org/schema/
security"
    xmlns:beans="http://www.springframework.org
/schema/beans"
    xmlns:xsi="http://www.w3.org/2001/XMLSchema-instance"
    xsi:schemaLocation="http://www.springframework.org
/schema/beans
    http://www.springframework.org/schema/beans/spring-
beans-3.0.xsd
    http://www.springframework.org/schema/security
    http://www.springframework.org/schema/security/spring-
security-3.1.xsd">

  <global-method-security pre-post-annotations="enabled">
        <!-- AspectJ pointcut expression that locates our "post"
method and applies security that way
```

```
        <protect-pointcut expression="execution(*
bigbank.*Service.post*(..))" access="ROLE_TELLER"/>
        -->
    </global-method-security>
    <http auto-config="true" use-expressions="true" >
        <intercept-url pattern="/welcome" access="hasRole('ROLE_
ADMIN')"/>
<!--         <intercept-url pattern="/admin"
access="hasRole('ROLE_admin')"/> -->


        <form-login login-page="/login" default-target-
url="/secure/common.jsp" authentication-failure-url="/
loginfailed?error=true" />

<authentication-manager>
        <ldap-authentication-provider
                        user-search-filter="(mail={0})"
                        user-search-base="ou=people"
                        group-search-
filter="(uniqueMember={0})"
                group-search-base="ou=groups"
                group-role-attribute="cn"
                role-prefix="ROLE_">
        </ldap-authentication-provider>
    </authentication-manager>

    <ldap-server url="ldap://localhost:10389/o=sevenSeas"
manager-dn="uid=admin,ou=system" manager-password="secret"
/>
</beans:beans>
```

How it works...

`Spring Security-ldap.xml` will contain details on the server location and the domain. It should connect to retrieve the user information. The domain is `sevenSeas`. 1039 is the port number for the LDAP server. Spring Security uses the `ldap-server` tag to give the information on LDAP. It also gives the password and the domain on which it will connect. The Struts 2 request will be interrupted by Spring Security and, for authentication, the user information will be received from the login page. Spring Security requires the LDAP for the username; on success, the user is given access to the secured resources.

See also

▶ *Chapter 3, Spring Security with JSF*

3
Spring Security with JSF

In this chapter we will cover:

- ▶ Integrating JSF with Spring Security
- ▶ JSF with form-based Spring Security
- ▶ JSF and form-based authentication using Spring Security to display logged-in user
- ▶ Using JSF with digest/hashing-based Spring Security
- ▶ Logging out with JSF using Spring Security
- ▶ Authenticating database with Spring Security and JSF
- ▶ ApacheDS authentication with JSF and Spring Security
- ▶ Authentication error message with JSF and Spring Security

Introduction

There are many applications developed in Apache Faces/JSF. It's not an action oriented framework like Struts 2, but purely meant for the view layer. To implement Spring Security with JSF, we need to figure out some work around. Let's see some recipes with respect to JSF and Spring Security.

I have used the latest stable version of Spring Security and Spring-core. If you want to do an update with your libraries, you can read the following section. For Maven users, it's all about updating the dependencies and for the normal Eclipse users, it's about adding the .jar files to the lib folder.

Setting up JSF application on Eclipse

1. Use Eclipse Java EE developer tools and set up a dynamic web project.

2. Give project name: `JSf_Spring_Security_Chapter_3_Recipe1`.

3. Select a dynamic web module Version 2.5.

4. Configurations: JavaServer Faces v1.2 project.

5. In the next **New Dynamic Web Project** window, click on **Download library**.

6. Select the Apache MyFaces lib.

Spring Security MAJOR/MINOR/PATCH versions

When I was setting up security for my applications, I faced a lot of errors with the schema versioning.

Spring source gives a good description about which version to download. It suggests that the PATCH version is the safest and will not affect the existing code, since it will use backward compatibility. The MINOR version comes with the design changes and MAJOR version comes with major API changes. For the JSF recipe I have been using 3.1.4 security version and I have downloaded Spring-3.1.4 related JARs.

You can download spring-security-3.1.4.RELEASE-dist, which comes with all the latest JARs.

JARs:

 ▸ `spring-security-config` does the namespace parsing and will read the `spring-security.xml` file

 ▸ Spring Security web interacts with the web application filters

 ▸ Spring Security core

Save these JARs in your `WEB-INF/lib` folder of your web application.

Integrating JSF with Spring Security

Let's create a simple Apache MyFaces application in Eclipse. Also let's integrate Spring Security to JSF, and then demonstrate basic authentication.

Getting ready

 ▸ You will need Eclipse Indigo or a higher version

 ▸ Create a dynamic web project JSF

 ▸ In your Eclipse IDE, create a dynamic web project: `JSf_Spring_Security_Chapter_3_Recipe1`

- ▸ Create a source folder: `src/main/java`
- ▸ Create a package: `com.packt.jsf.bean`
- ▸ Create a Managed Bean: `User.java`
- ▸ Use Tomcat server to deploy the application

How to do it...

Perform the following steps to implement a basic authentication mechanism with JSF and Spring Security:

1. `User.java` is the Managed Bean of the application. It has two methods: `sayHello()` and `reset()`:

   `User.java` class:

```java
package com.packt.jsf.bean;
public class User {
    private String name;
    private boolean flag= true;
    public String getName() {
        return this.name;
    }
    public void setName(String name) {
        this.name = name;
    }
     public String  sayHello(){
         flag= false;
         name="Hello "+ name;
        return this.name;

    }
     public String  reset(){
         flag= true;
         name=null;
        return "reset";

    }
    public boolean isFlag() {
        return flag;
    }

    public void setFlag(boolean flag) {
        this.flag = flag;
    }
}
```

2. Let's create a JSP file, which is based on the `ApacheMyFaces` tags. It expects a mandatory `<f:view>` tag. It's a convention to create a JSP file with the same name as its bean. It has a form which accepts the name and says **"hello"** on clicking the button:

`User.jsp`:

```jsp
<%@ page language="java" contentType="text/html;
charset=ISO-8859-1" pageEncoding="ISO-8859-1"%>
<%@ taglib prefix="f"  uri="http://java.sun.com/jsf/core"%>
<%@ taglib prefix="h"  uri="http://java.sun.com/jsf/html"%>
<!DOCTYPE html PUBLIC "-//W3C//DTD HTML 4.01 Transitional//EN"
"http://www.w3.org/TR/html4/loose.dtd">
<html>
<head>
<meta http-equiv="Content-Type" content="text/html;
charset=ISO-8859-1">
<title>User</title>
</head>
<body>
<f:view>
   <h:form>
     <h:panelGrid columns="2">
       <h:outputLabel value="Name"></h:outputLabel>
       <h:inputText   value="#{user.name}"></h:inputText>
     </h:panelGrid>
     <h:commandButton action="#{user.sayHello}"
value="sayHello"></h:commandButton>
     <h:commandButton action="#{user.reset}"
value="Reset"></h:commandButton>
        <h:messages layout="table"></h:messages>
   </h:form>


   <h:panelGroup rendered="#{user.flag!=true}">
   <h3> Result </h3>
   <h:outputLabel value="Welcome "></h:outputLabel>
   <h:outputLabel value="#{user.name}"></h:outputLabel>
   </h:panelGroup>
</f:view>
</body>
</html>
```

3. Update the `faces-config.xml` file with the Managed Bean:

```xml
<?xml version="1.0" encoding="UTF-8"?>
<faces-config
    xmlns="http://java.sun.com/xml/ns/javaee"
```

```
    xmlns:xsi="http://www.w3.org/2001/XMLSchema-instance"
    xsi:schemaLocation="http://java.sun.com/xml/ns/javaee
http://java.sun.com/xml/ns/javaee/web-facesconfig_1_2.xsd"
    version="1.2">
    <application>

        <el-resolver>org.springframework.web.jsf
.el.SpringBeanFacesELResolver</el-resolver>
        <!--
        <variable-resolver>org.springframework.web.jsf.
SpringBeanVariableResolver</variable-resolver>
        -->
    </application>
    <managed-bean>
        <managed-bean-name>user</managed-bean-name>
        <managed-bean-
class>com.packt.jsf.bean.User</managed-bean-class>
        <managed-bean-scope>session</managed-bean-scope>
    </managed-bean>

</faces-config>
```

4. The `Spring-security.xml` file remains the same but I have used the latest jar- 3.1.4 security jars:

```
<beans:beans xmlns="http://www.springframework.org/schema/
security" xmlns:beans="http://www.springframework.org/schema/
beans" xmlns:xsi="http://www.w3.org/2001/XMLSchema-instance"
xsi:schemaLocation="http://www.springframework.org/schema/beans
http://www.springframework.org/schema/beans/spring-beans-3.0.xsd
 http://www.springframework.org/schema/security
 http://www.springframework.org/schema/security/spring-security-
3.1.xsd">

 <global-method-security pre-post-annotations="enabled">

    </global-method-security>
    <http auto-config="true" use-expressions="true" >
        <intercept-url pattern="/faces/User.jsp"
access="hasRole('ROLE_DIRECTOR')"/>
        <http-basic />
    </http>
    <authentication-manager>
      <authentication-provider>
        <user-service>
```

```
                    <user name="packt" password="123456" authorities="ROLE_
    DIRECTOR" />
            </user-service>
        </authentication-provider>
      </authentication-manager>
    </beans:beans>
```

5. The `web.xml` file should be updated with Spring filters and listeners. It also has configurations of MyFaces:

```
Spring-security.xml:
```

```xml
<?xml version="1.0" encoding="UTF-8"?>
<web-app xmlns:xsi="http://www.w3.org/2001/XMLSchema-
instance" xmlns="http://java.sun.com/xml/ns/javaee"
xmlns:web="http://java.sun.com/xml/ns/javaee/web-
app_2_5.xsd"
xsi:schemaLocation="http://java.sun.com/xml/ns/javaee
http://java.sun.com/xml/ns/javaee/web-app_2_5.xsd"
id="WebApp_ID" version="2.5">
  <display-name>JSf_Spring_Security_Chapter_3_Recipe1
</display-name>
  <welcome-file-list>
    <welcome-file>index.jsp</welcome-file>
  </welcome-file-list>

  <context-param>
    <param-name>contextConfigLocation</param-name>
    <param-value>
          /WEB-INF/spring-security.xml

        </param-value>
  </context-param>
 <filter>
    <filter-name>springSecurityFilterChain</filter-name>
    <filter-class>
  org.springframework.web.filter.DelegatingFilterProxy
              </filter-class>
  </filter>
  <filter-mapping>
    <filter-name>springSecurityFilterChain</filter-name>
    <url-pattern>/*</url-pattern>
  </filter-mapping>
  <listener>
    <listener-class>org.springframework.web.
context.ContextLoaderListener</listener-class>
```

```
    </listener>
    <servlet>
      <servlet-name>Faces Servlet</servlet-name>
      <servlet-class>javax.faces.webapp.FacesServlet
</servlet-class>
      <load-on-startup>1</load-on-startup>
    </servlet>
    <servlet-mapping>
      <servlet-name>Faces Servlet</servlet-name>
      <url-pattern>/faces/*</url-pattern>
    </servlet-mapping>
    <context-param>
      <param-name>javax.servlet.jsp.jstl.fmt.
localizationContext</param-name>
      <param-value>resources.application</param-value>
    </context-param>
    <context-param>
      <description>State saving method: 'client' or 'server'
(=default). See JSF Specification 2.5.2</description>
      <param-name>javax.faces.STATE_SAVING_METHOD
</param-name>
      <param-value>client</param-value>
    </context-param>
    <context-param>
      <description>
    This parameter tells MyFaces if javascript code should be
allowed in
      the rendered HTML output.
    If javascript is allowed, command_link anchors will
have javascript code
      that submits the corresponding form.
    If javascript is not allowed, the state saving info and
nested parameters
      will be added as url parameters.
    Default is 'true'</description>
      <param-name>org.apache.myfaces.ALLOW_JAVASCRIPT</param-name>
      <param-value>true</param-value>
    </context-param>
    <context-param>
      <description>
    If true, rendered HTML code will be formatted, so that it is
'human-readable'
    i.e. additional line separators and whitespace will be written,
that do not
      influence the HTML code.
```

```
        Default is 'true'</description>
          <param-name>org.apache.myfaces.PRETTY_HTML</param-name>
          <param-value>true</param-value>
      </context-param>
      <context-param>
        <param-name>org.apache.myfaces.DETECT_JAVASCRIPT</param-name>
        <param-value>false</param-value>
      </context-param>
      <context-param>
        <description>
        If true, a javascript function will be rendered that is able to
    restore the
        former vertical scroll on every request. Convenient feature if
    you have pages
        with long lists and you do not want the browser page to always
    jump to the top
        if you trigger a link or button action that stays on the same
    page.
        Default is 'false'
    </description>
          <param-name>org.apache.myfaces.AUTO_SCROLL</param-name>
          <param-value>true</param-value>
      </context-param>
      <listener>
        <listener-class>org.apache.myfaces.webapp.
    StartupServletContextListener</listener-class>
      </listener>
    </web-app>:beans>
```

How it works...

When the user tries to access the secured `user.jsp` page, Spring Security intercepts the URL and redirects the user to the login page. On successful authentication, the user is redirected to the success `url` mentioned in the `spring-security.xml` file. The following screenshots show the workflow of implementing basic authentication with JSF and Spring Security.

Now access the following URL: `http://localhost:8086/JSf_Spring_Security_Chapter_3_Recipe1/faces/User.jsp`.

You should see a basic authentication dialog box asking you to log in as shown in the following screenshot:

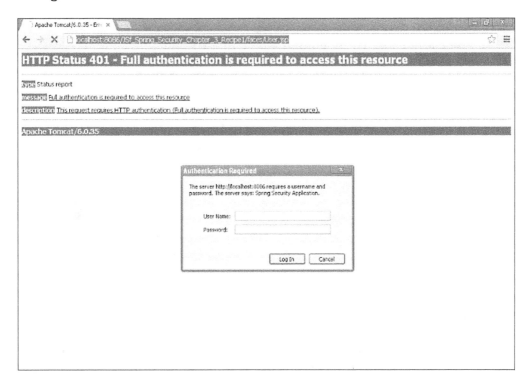

The following screenshot is the secured page of JSF, which can be accessed after successful authentication:

See also

▶ The *JSF with form-based Spring Security* recipe

▶ The *JSF and form-based authentication using Spring Security to display logged-in user* recipe

▶ The *Using JSF with digest/hashing-based Spring Security* recipe

▶ The *Logging out with JSF using Spring Security* recipe

▶ The *Authenticating database with Spring Security and JSF* recipe

▶ The *ApacheDS authentication with JSF and Spring Security* recipe

▶ The *Authentication error message with JSF and Spring Security* recipe

JSF with form-based Spring Security

In this section we will implement the form-based authentication with JSF and Spring Security. Integrating Apache MyFaces with Spring Security is not as simple as Struts 2 integration.

It needs a work around. The `/j_spring_security` method can't be understood by ApacheMyfaces. The work around is to create a custom login method in our Managed Bean class. We will use the JSF external context class to pass the authentication request to the Spring Security Framework.

Getting ready

▶ Create a new project in you Eclipse IDE: `JSF_Spring_Security_Chapter_3_Recipe2`

▶ Do the configurations as shown in the following screenshot

▶ Create a package: `com.packt.jsf.beans`

How to do it...

Perform the following steps to integrate JSF with Spring Security to implement form-based authentication:

1. Create a web project in Eclipse:

2. Create a Credential Manager Bean:

    This bean has all the properties of a form-based authentication bean and customized login method ();

    The j_username and j_password values will be set and the user is displayed in the secured page.

The doSpringSecurityLogin() bean: Just like we access ServletContext and we bind it with the request dispatcher, we can use ExternalContext with request dispatcher to execute the /j_spring_security_check.

The phaseListener implementation is meant to capture the authentication exceptions.

CredentialManager.java:

```java
public class CredentialManager implements PhaseListener{
    private String j_username;
    private String j_password;

     public String getJ_password() {
         return j_password;
    }
    public void setJ_password(String j_password) {
         this.j_password = j_password;
    }
    public String doSpringSecurityLogin() throws
      IOException, ServletException
        {
            ExternalContext context = FacesContext.
              getCurrentInstance().getExternalContext();
            RequestDispatcher dispatcher = ((ServletRequest)
              context.getRequest()).getRequestDispatcher
              ("/j_spring_security_check");
            dispatcher.forward((ServletRequest)
              context.getRequest(),(ServletResponse)
              context.getResponse());
            FacesContext.getCurrentInstance().
              responseComplete();
            return null;
        }
    public String getJ_username() {
         return j_username;
    }
    public void setJ_username(String j_username) {
         this.j_username = j_username;
    }
    @Override
    public void afterPhase(PhaseEvent arg0) {
         // TODO Auto-generated method stub

    }
    @Override
```

```
public void beforePhase(PhaseEvent event) {
        Exception e = (Exception) FacesContext.
          getCurrentInstance().getExternalContext()
          .getSessionMap().get(
        WebAttributes.AUTHENTICATION_EXCEPTION);

        if (e instanceof BadCredentialsException) {
            System.out.println("error block"+e);
            FacesContext.getCurrentInstance()
              .getExternalContext().getSessionMap().put(
                WebAttributes.AUTHENTICATION_EXCEPTION,
                  null);
            FacesContext.getCurrentInstance()
              .addMessage(null, new FacesMessage
              (FacesMessage.SEVERITY_ERROR,"Username or
              password not valid.", "Username or
              password not valid"));
        }
    }

    @Override
    public PhaseId getPhaseId() {
            return PhaseId.RENDER_RESPONSE;
    }
}
```

3. Let's update the `Spring-security.xml` file. The `login-processing-url` is mapped to `j_security_check`:

```
<beans:beans xmlns="http://www.springframework.org
/schema/security" xmlns:beans="http://www.springframework
.org/schema/beans" xmlns:xsi="http://www.w3.org/2001/
XMLSchema-instance" xsi:schemaLocation="http:
//www.springframework.org/schema/beans http://
www.springframework.org/schema/beans/spring-beans-3.0.xsd
 http://www.springframework.org/schema/security
  http://www.springframework.org/schema/security/spring-
security-3.1.xsd">

 <global-method-security pre-post-annotations="enabled">

   </global-method-security>
   <http auto-config="true" use-expressions="true" >

        <intercept-url pattern="/faces/Supplier.jsp"
          access="hasRole('ROLE_USER')"/>
```

```
            <form-login login-processing-
              url="/j_spring_security_check" login-
              page="/faces/login.jsp" default-target-
              url="/faces/Supplier.jsp" authentication-
              failure-url="/faces/login.jsp" />
            <logout/>
      </http>

      <authentication-manager>
        <authentication-provider>
          <user-service>
            <user name="anjana" password="anju123456"
              authorities="ROLE_USER"/>
          </user-service>
        </authentication-provider>
      </authentication-manager>
  </beans: beans>
```

4. Add the Managed Bean into the `faces-config.xml` file:

```
<?xml version="1.0" encoding="UTF-8"?>

<faces-config
    xmlns="http://java.sun.com/xml/ns/javaee"
    xmlns:xsi="http://www.w3.org/2001/XMLSchema-instance"
    xsi:schemaLocation="http://java.sun.com/xml/ns/javaee
      http://java.sun.com/xml/ns/javaee/web-
      facesconfig_1_2.xsd"
    version="1.2">
    <lifecycle>
        <phase-listener>com.packt.jsf.beans.
          CredentialManager</phase-listener>
    </lifecycle>
     <application>

        <el-resolver>org.springframework.web.
          jsf.el.SpringBeanFacesELResolver</el-resolver>
        <!--
        <variable-resolver>org.springframework.web.
          jsf.SpringBeanVariableResolver</variable-
          resolver>
        -->
    </application>

        <managed-bean>
        <managed-bean-name>credentialmanager</managed-
          bean-name>
```

```
        <managed-bean-class>com.packt.jsf.beans.
          CredentialManager</managed-bean-class>
        <managed-bean-scope>session</managed-bean-scope>
    </managed-bean>


    </faces-config>
```

5. Now comes the `login.jsp` file for Apache MyFaces.

    The `login.jsp` file should have the following:

    > `prependID=false`

    > It should submit to the custom login method defined in the `ManagedBean`

```
<%@ page language="java" contentType="text/html;
charset=ISO-8859-1" pageEncoding="ISO-8859-1"%>
<%@ taglib prefix="f" uri="http://java.sun.com/jsf/core"%>
<%@ taglib prefix="h" uri="http://java.sun.com/jsf/html"%>
<!DOCTYPE html PUBLIC "-//W3C//DTD HTML 4.01 Transitional//EN"
"http://www.w3.org/TR/html4/loose.dtd">
<html>
<head>
<meta http-equiv="Content-Type" content="text/html;
charset=ISO-8859-1">
<title>Spring Security Login</title>
</head>
<body>
<f:view>
<h:form prependId="false">
<h:panelGrid columns="2">
<h:outputLabel value="j_username"></h:outputLabel>
<h:inputText   id="j_username" required="true"
value="#{credentialmanager.j_username}"></h:inputText>
<h:outputLabel value="j_password"></h:outputLabel>
<h:inputSecret  id ="j_password" required="true"
value="#{credentialmanager.j_password}"></h:inputSecret>
</h:panelGrid>
<h:commandButton action="#{credentialmanager.
doSpringSecurityLogin}" value="SpringSecurityLogin"/>
  </h:form>
</f:view>
</body>
</html>
```

How it works...

Access the following URL: `localhost:8086/JSF_Spring_Security_Chapter_3_Recipe2/faces/Supplier.jsp`.

When the user accesses the URL, they will be redirected to the login page. The user then enters their credentials and clicks on **Submit**. The `ExternalContext` object is instantiated using the `FacesContext` object using the `PhaseListener` implementation. The `context` object is passed to the request object with `'j_spring_security_check'` URL. The Spring Security will do the authentication and authorization. On authentication failure, an exception is thrown.

See also

- The *JSF and form-based authentication using Spring Security to display logged-in user* recipe
- The *Using JSF with digest/hashing-based Spring Security* recipe
- The *Logging out with JSF using Spring Security* recipe
- The *Authenticating database with Spring Security and JSF* recipe
- The *ApacheDS authentication with JSF and Spring Security* recipe
- The *Authentication error message with JSF and Spring Security* recipe

JSF and form-based authentication using Spring Security to display logged-in user

In the previous recipe, we demonstrated the implementation of form-based authentication using Spring Security and JSF `phaseListener`. In this section we will display the logged in user.

Getting ready

You have to perform some minor changes in the `Supplier.jsp` file.

How do it...

Perform the following steps to display the logged in user details on the browser:

1. To display the logged in user, access the managed bean object in your secured page.

2. In the `Supplier.jsp` file, edit the following:

```
<%@ page language="java" contentType="text/html;
charset=ISO-8859-1" pageEncoding="ISO-8859-1"%>
```

```
<%@ taglib prefix="f" uri="http://java.sun.com/jsf/core"%>
<%@ taglib prefix="h" uri="http://java.sun.com/jsf/html"%>
<!DOCTYPE html PUBLIC "-//W3C//DTD HTML 4.01
Transitional//EN" "http://www.w3.org/TR/html4/loose.dtd">
<html>
<head>
<meta http-equiv="Content-Type" content="text/html;
charset=ISO-8859-1">
<title>Insert title here</title>
</head>
<body>
<f:view>
<h:panelGroup>
  <h3> Result </h3>
  <h:outputLabel value="Welcome "></h:outputLabel>
  <h:outputLabel value="#{credentialmanager.j_username}">
    </h:outputLabel>
  </h:panelGroup>
</f:view>
</body>
</html>
```

How it works...

When the user is redirected to the login page the faces context object submits the user information to Spring Security. On success the user POJO's getters and setters sets the user information, which is used to display the user information on the JSP page.

The following screenshot shows the workflow for displaying the user information in the browser using JSF and Spring Security with form-based authentication:

On successful authentication, the user will be directed to the following page:

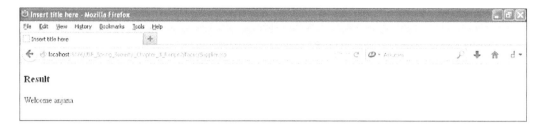

- ▶ The *Using JSF with digest/hashing-based Spring Security* recipe
- ▶ The *Logging out with JSF using Spring Security* recipe
- ▶ The *Authenticating database with Spring Security and JSF* recipe
- ▶ The *ApacheDS authentication with JSF and Spring Security* recipe
- ▶ The *Authentication error message with JSF and Spring Security* recipe

Using JSF with digest/hashing-based Spring Security

In this section we will implement digest authentication with JSF and Spring Security. The user's password is hashed using one of the encryption algorithms and configured in the `.xml` file. The algorithm used to hash the password is also mentioned in the configuration file.

Getting ready

Spring digest authentication works fine with JSF as well. We need to hash the password using `jacksum.jar`. Provide the hashed password in the configuration file. Also mention the algorithm used for hashing in the configuration file.

How to do it...

Perform the following steps for implementing the digest authentication mechanism with JSF and Spring Security:

1. Let's encrypt the password: `packt123456`.
2. We need to use an external jar, Jacksum, which means Java checksum.
3. It supports both MD5 and SHA1 encryption.

4. Download the `jacksum.zip` file and extract the ZIP folder.

```
packt>java -jar jacksum.jar -a sha -q"txt:packt123456"
```

5. Let's create a new project to demonstrate this and we will use basic authentication. Create a dynamic web project in Eclipse and name it `JSF_Spring_Security_DIGEST_Recipe3`.

6. The `web.xml`, `face-config.xml`, and JSP settings remain the same as the `JSF_Spring_Security_Chapter3_Recipe1`. We need to update the `Spring-security.xml` file to authenticate using the SHA encryption and decryption:

`Spring-security.xml`:

```
<beans:beans
xmlns="http://www.springframework.org/schema/security"
xmlns:beans="http://www.springframework.org/schema/beans"
xmlns:xsi="http://www.w3.org/2001/XMLSchema-instance"
xsi:schemaLocation="http://www.springframework.org/schema/b
eans http://www.springframework.org/schema/beans/spring-
beans-3.0.xsd
 http://www.springframework.org/schema/security
 http://www.springframework.org/schema/security/spring-
security-3.1.xsd">

 <global-method-security pre-post-annotations="enabled">

   </global-method-security>
   <http auto-config="true" use-expressions="true" >
       <intercept-url pattern="/faces/User.jsp"
         access="hasRole('ROLE_DIRECTOR')"/>
       <http-basic />
   </http>

   <authentication-manager>
     <authentication-provider>
   <password-encoder hash="sha" />
     <user-service>
       <user name="anjana" password=
         "bde892ed4e131546a2f9997cc94d31e2c8f18b2a"
           authorities="ROLE_DIRECTOR" />
     </user-service>
   </authentication-provider>
   </authentication-manager>
</beans:beans>
```

How it works...

When you run the application, you will be prompted with a dialog box.

On entering the username and password, the Spring Framework will decrypt the password and will compare it with the user's entered details. When they match, it flags an authentication success message, which will make the context object redirect the user to the success URL.

The following screenshots show the workflow of digest authentication with JSF and Spring.

It is a basic form but the authentication mechanism is digest.

Spring has authenticated the user by decrypting the password:

See also

- ▸ The *Logging out with JSF using Spring Security* recipe
- ▸ The *Authenticating database with Spring Security and JSF* recipe
- ▸ The *ApacheDS authentication with JSF and Spring Security* recipe
- ▸ The *Authentication error message with JSF and Spring Security* recipe

Logging out with JSF using Spring Security

In this section, we will implement the logging out scenario using Spring Security in a JSF application.

Getting ready

- Implement the `PhaseListener` class
- Add a `commandButton` on the JSF page

How to do it...

Perform the following steps for implementing Spring Security logout in a JSF application:

1. Create a **New Dynamic Web Project** in your Eclipse:

2. We will create a `CredentialManager` bean again. It will have another custom logout method. `Login.jsp` remains the same as the previous example. Do not forget to copy it into the new project. We will use form-based authentication here:

```
package com.packt.jsf.beans;

import java.io.IOException;

import javax.faces.context.ExternalContext;
import javax.faces.context.FacesContext;
import javax.faces.event.PhaseEvent;
import javax.faces.event.PhaseId;
import javax.faces.event.PhaseListener;
import org.springframework.security.
  authentication.BadCredentialsException;
import javax.faces.application.FacesMessage;

import org.springframework.security.web.WebAttributes;

public class CredentialManager implements PhaseListener{
    /**
     *
     */
    private static final long serialVersionUID = 1L;
    private String j_username;
    private String j_password;

     public String getJ_password() {
          return j_password;
    }
    public void setJ_password(String j_password) {
          this.j_password = j_password;
    }
    public String doSpringSecurityLogin() throws IOException,
      ServletException
        {
            ExternalContext context = FacesContext.
              getCurrentInstance().getExternalContext();
            RequestDispatcher dispatcher = ((ServletRequest)
              context.getRequest()).getRequestDispatcher
              ("/j_spring_security_check");
            dispatcher.forward((ServletRequest)
              context.getRequest(),(ServletResponse)
              context.getResponse());
            FacesContext.getCurrentInstance()
              .responseComplete();
```

```
              return null;
        }
    public String doSpringSecurityLogout() throws IOException,
      ServletException
     {
        ExternalContext context = FacesContext.
          getCurrentInstance().getExternalContext();
        RequestDispatcher dispatcher = ((ServletRequest)
          context.getRequest()).getRequestDispatcher
          ("/j_spring_security_logout");
        dispatcher.forward((ServletRequest)
          context.getRequest(),(ServletResponse)
          context.getResponse());
        FacesContext.getCurrentInstance().responseComplete();
        return null;
     }
    public String getJ_username() {
          return j_username;
    }
    public void setJ_username(String j_username) {
          this.j_username = j_username;
    }
    public void afterPhase(PhaseEvent arg0) {
          // TODO Auto-generated method stub

    }
    public void beforePhase(PhaseEvent arg0) {
          Exception e = (Exception) FacesContext.
            getCurrentInstance().getExternalContext()
            .getSessionMap().get(
            WebAttributes.AUTHENTICATION_EXCEPTION);

          if (e instanceof BadCredentialsException) {
              System.out.println("error block"+e);
              FacesContext.getCurrentInstance()
                .getExternalContext().getSessionMap().put(
                  WebAttributes.AUTHENTICATION_EXCEPTION,
                    null);
              FacesContext.getCurrentInstance().
                addMessage(null, new FacesMessage
                (FacesMessage.SEVERITY_ERROR,"Username or
                password not valid.", "Username or
                password not valid"));
          }
    }
```

```
        public PhaseId getPhaseId() {
                return PhaseId.RENDER_RESPONSE;
        }

}
```

3. Let's provide a **Logout** button in our secured page:

`Supplier.jsp`:

```
<%@ page language="java" contentType="text/html;
charset=ISO-8859-1" pageEncoding="ISO-8859-1"%>
<%@ taglib prefix="f"  uri="http://java.sun.com/jsf/core"%>
<%@ taglib prefix="h"  uri="http://java.sun.com/jsf/html"%>
<!DOCTYPE html PUBLIC "-//W3C//DTD HTML 4.01 Transitional//EN"
"http://www.w3.org/TR/html4/loose.dtd">
<html>
<head>
<meta http-equiv="Content-Type" content="text/html;
charset=ISO-8859-1">
<title>Insert title here</title>
</head>
<body>
<f:view>
   <h:form prependId="false">
<h:panelGroup>
   <h:outputLabel value="Welcome "></h:outputLabel>
   <h:outputLabel value="#{credentialmanager.j_username}"></
h:outputLabel>
   </h:panelGroup>

   <h:commandButton action="#{credentialmanager.
doSpringSecurityLogout}" value="SpringSecurityLogout" />
   </h:form>
</f:view>
</body>
</html>
```

4. Update the `Spring-security.xml` file:

```
<beans:beans
xmlns="http://www.springframework.org/schema/security"
xmlns:beans="http://www.springframework.org/schema/beans"
xmlns:xsi="http://www.w3.org/2001/XMLSchema-instance"
xsi:schemaLocation="http://www.springframework.org/schema/b
eans http://www.springframework.org/schema/beans/spring-
beans-3.0.xsd
```

```
http://www.springframework.org/schema/security
  http://www.springframework.org/schema/security/spring-
security-3.1.xsd">

<global-method-security pre-post-annotations="enabled">

  </global-method-security>
  <http auto-config="true" use-expressions="true" >

      <intercept-url pattern="/faces/Supplier.jsp"
        access="hasRole('ROLE_USER')"/>
      <form-login login-processing-
        url="/j_spring_security_check" login-
        page="/faces/login.jsp" default-target-
        url="/faces/Supplier.jsp" authentication-
        failure-url="/faces/login.jsp" />
      <logout  logout-success-url="/faces/login.jsp" />
  </http>

  <authentication-manager>
    <authentication-provider>
      <user-service>
        <user name="anjana" password="123456"
          authorities="ROLE_USER"/>
      </user-service>
    </authentication-provider>
  </authentication-manager>
</beans:beans>
```

How it works...

The `CredentialManager` class implements the `phaseListener interface`. The `doSpringSecurityLogout` method handles the Spring logout by creating a context object using `ExternalContext`. The context then submits the logout request that is `"/j_spring_ security_logout"` to the Spring Security Framework, which logs out the user.

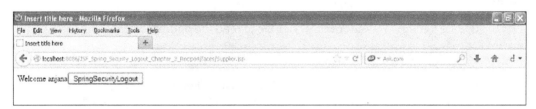

On clicking on logout, the user is redirected to the login page.

See also

 ▸ The *Authenticating database with Spring Security and JSF* recipe

 ▸ The *ApacheDS authentication with JSF and Spring Security* recipe

 ▸ The *Authentication error message with JSF and Spring Security* recipe

Authenticating database with Spring Security and JSF

In this section, we will use the database to authenticate users with Spring Security in a JSF application. We have referred to the logout example and have used the database for authentication.

Getting ready

 ▸ Create a dynamic web project in Eclipse: `JSF_Spring_DBAuthentication_Recipe6`

 ▸ All the files and folders remain the same as the logout application

 ▸ Update the `security.xml` file and the `web.xml` file

 ▸ Add the following JARs into the `lib` folder or update your POM file if you are using Maven:

   ❏ spring-jdbc-3.1.4RELEASE

   ❏ mysql-connector-java-5.1.17-bin

   ❏ commons-dbcp

   ❏ commons-pool-1.5.4

How to do it...

The following steps will help us to authenticate the user information by retrieving data from the database:

1. Update the `Spring-security.xml` file to read the database configuration:

   `applicationContext-security.xml`:

   ```
   <beans: beans
   xmlns="http://www.springframework.org/schema/security"
   xmlns:beans="http://www.springframework.org/schema/beans"
   xmlns:xsi="http://www.w3.org/2001/XMLSchema-instance"
   xsi:schemaLocation="http://www.springframework.org/schema/b
   eans http://www.springframework.org/schema/beans/spring-
   beans-3.0.xsd
   ```

```
http://www.springframework.org/schema/security
 http://www.springframework.org/schema/security/spring-
security-3.1.xsd">

<global-method-security pre-post-annotations="enabled">

  </global-method-security>
  <http auto-config="true" use-expressions="true" >

        <intercept-url pattern="/faces/Supplier.jsp"
          access="hasRole('ROLE_USER')"/>
       <form-login login-processing-
         url="/j_spring_security_check" login-
         page="/faces/login.jsp" default-target-
         url="/faces/Supplier.jsp" authentication-
         failure-url="/faces/login.jsp" />
       <logout  logout-success-url="/faces/login.jsp" />

  </http>

  <authentication-manager>
     <authentication-provider>
        <jdbc-user-service data-source-ref="MySqlDS"
          users-by-username-query="
            select username,password, enabled
            from users1 where username=?"

          authorities-by-username-query="
            select u.username, ur.role from users1 u,
            user_roles ur
        where u.user_id = ur.user_id and u.username =?  " />
     </authentication-provider>
        </authentication-manager>
    </beans: beans>
```

How it works...

The data source reference is given in the `Sping-security.xml` file. When the user
clicks on **Login**, the Spring Security filter will invoke the database authentication related
classes, which will read the `db-beans.xml` file to establish the connection. The `<jdbc-
user-service>` tag implements the database authentication by executing the query and
retrieving the user information from the database based on the parameter submitted by the
user in the browser.

See also

▶ The *ApacheDS authentication with JSF and Spring Security* recipe

▶ The *Authentication error message with JSF and Spring Security* recipe

ApacheDS authentication with JSF and Spring Security

In this section, we will authenticate users in the JSF application using ApacheDS and Spring Security.

Getting ready

ApacheDS authentication is similar to Struts 2 ApacheDS authentication:

▶ Create a dynamic web project in Eclipse: `JSF_Spring_ApacheDSAuthentication_Recipe7`

▶ All the files and folders remain the same as the logout application

▶ Update the `security.xml` file

▶ Add `spring-security-ldap.jar` to your `web-inf/lib` folder

How to do it...

Perform the following steps for configuring LDAP with Spring and the JSF application:

1. Update the `Spring-security.xml` file to read the LDAP configuration:

```
<beans:beans
xmlns="http://www.springframework.org/schema/security"
xmlns:beans="http://www.springframework.org/schema/beans"
xmlns:xsi="http://www.w3.org/2001/XMLSchema-instance"
xsi:schemaLocation="http://www.springframework.org/schema/b
eans http://www.springframework.org/schema/beans/spring-
beans-3.0.xsd
 http://www.springframework.org/schema/security
  http://www.springframework.org/schema/security/spring-
security-3.1.xsd">

 <global-method-security pre-post-annotations="enabled">

   </global-method-security>
   <http auto-config="true" use-expressions="true" >
```

```
            <intercept-url pattern="/faces/Supplier.jsp"
               access="hasRole('ROLE_USER')"/>
          <form-login login-processing-
url="/j_spring_security_check" login-
page="/faces/login.jsp" default-target-
url="/faces/Supplier.jsp" authentication-failure-
url="/faces/login.jsp" />
          <logout  logout-success-url="/faces/login.jsp" />
             </http>
          <authentication-manager>
            <ldap-authentication-provider
                            user-search-filter="(mail={0})"
                            user-search-base="ou=people"
                            group-search-
                               filter="(uniqueMember={0})"
                     group-search-base="ou=groups"
                     group-role-attribute="cn"
                     role-prefix="ROLE_">
            </ldap-authentication-provider>
       </authentication-manager>

    <ldap-server url="ldap://localhost:389/o=example"
manager-dn="uid=admin,ou=system" manager-password="secret"
/></beans:beans>
```

How it works...

The JSF filters are used for delegation. Spring filters are used for authentication. We have used ldap-authentication-provider for setting the LDAP parameters to the Spring Security engine. When the application receives a request for authentication and authorization, spring-security-ldap provider sets the LDAP parameters and connects with the LDAP using the ldap-server-url parameter. It then retrieves the user details and gives it to the Spring authentication manager and filter to handle the response of the authentication.

See also

▶ The *Authentication error message with JSF and Spring Security* recipe

Authentication error message with JSF and Spring Security

In this section, we will see how we can capture the authentication error message and display it to the user on the browser. The `credentialmanager` bean as displayed in the previous example will capture the authentication failure exceptions. We will see how to capture it in JSP.

Getting ready

The `credentialmanager` bean has captured the bad credential exception.

We need to display it to the user. This can be done by using the `<h: messages>` tag in our JSP file. This should be given inside the grid tag. The very purpose of implementing the `phaselistener` in Managed Bean is to capture the message and display it to the user. This is the updated `login.jsp`.

How to do it...

Perform the following steps to capture the authentication failure message in JSP:

▶ Edit the `login.jsp` file:

```
<!DOCTYPE html PUBLIC "-//W3C//DTD HTML 4.01
Transitional//EN" "http://www.w3.org/TR/html4/loose.dtd">
<%@ page language="java" contentType="text/html;
charset=ISO-8859-1" pageEncoding="ISO-8859-1"%>
<%@ taglib prefix="f"  uri="http://java.sun.com/jsf/core"%>
<%@ taglib prefix="h"  uri="http://java.sun.com/jsf/html"%>

<html>
<head>
<meta http-equiv="Content-Type" content="text/html;
charset=ISO-8859-1">
<title>Insert title here</title>
</head>
<body>
<f:view>
<h:form prependId="false">
              <h:panelGrid columns="2">

                  <h:outputLabel
                    value="j_username"></h:outputLabel>
```

```
              <h:inputText     id="j_username" required="true"
                value="#{credentialmanager.j_username}">
                </h:inputText>
                 <h:outputLabel value="j_password">
                    </h:outputLabel>
              <h:inputSecret     id ="j_password"
                required="true" value="#{credentialmanager
                .j_password}"></h:inputSecret>
                <h:outputLabel value="_spring_security_remember_
  me"></h:outputLabel>
                <h:selectBooleanCheckbox
                       id="_spring_security_remember_me" />

                </h:panelGrid>
                <h:commandButton action="#{credentialmanager.
  doSpringSecurityLogin}" value="SpringSecurityLogin" />
   <h:messages />


          </h:form>
          </f:view>
      </body>
      </html>
```

How it works...

The `beforePhase()` method in the `credentialmanager` captures the authentication exceptions message. The exception is added to `FacesMessage`, which is captured in the JSP file.

```
FacesContext.getCurrentInstance().addMessage(null, new
FacesMessage(FacesMessage.SEVERITY_ERROR,"Username or password not
valid.", "Username or password not valid"));
```

The following screenshot shows the implementation:

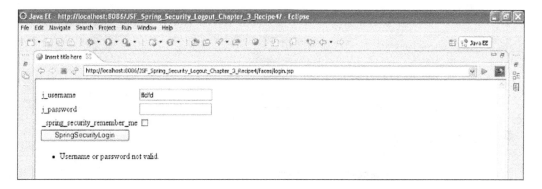

The following screenshot shows the screen on authentication failure:

The following screenshot shows the screen when empty credentials are entered in the username and password fields:

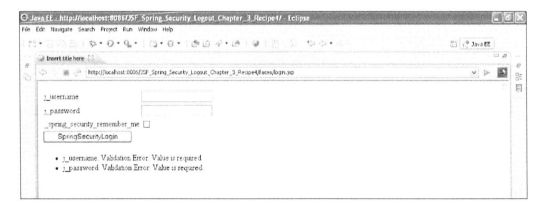

See also

▶ *Chapter 4, Spring Security with Grails*

4
Spring Security with Grails

In this chapter we will cover:

- ▶ Spring Security authentication with Groovy Grails setup
- ▶ Spring Security with Grails to Secure Grails controller
- ▶ Spring Security with Groovy Grails logout scenario
- ▶ Spring Security with Groovy Grails Basic authentication
- ▶ Spring Security with Groovy Grails Digest authentication
- ▶ Spring Security with Groovy Grails multiple authentication
- ▶ Spring Security with Groovy Grails LDAP authentication

Introduction

Grails is a plugin based framework and all it needs to work is a few intuitive commands on the command prompt.

In this chapter, we shall see how easily we can integrate Spring Security with Groovy on Grails with less coding.

Spring Security authentication with Groovy Grails setup

In this recipe we shall first set up Groovy and Grails. We shall then show how to integrate Spring Security with Grails.

Getting ready

- ▶ Get Groovy installed from http://groovy.codehaus.org/Download
- ▶ Download Grails 2.3 from http://groovy.codehaus.org/Download and unzip it to a folder
- ▶ Set environment variable: GRAILS_HOME
- ▶ Check for Groovy_HOME
- ▶ Check Grails installation by typing grails-version

How to do it...

The following steps are taken to integrate Spring Security with Groovy Grails:

1. Create a directory: Grails Project.

   ```
   cd Grails_Project
   grails create-app myfirstapp
   cd myfirstapp
   grails create-controller MyFirstController
   ```

   This will create a controller which will be available inside the controller package.

2. You can open the generated controller file and view it. It will have package name myfirstapp which Grails has auto generated.

   ```
   package myfirstapp
   class MyFirstController {
       def index() { }
   }
   ```

3. Update the generated controller file.

   ```
   package myfirstapp
   class MyFirstController {
     def index() {
       render "Hello PACKT"
     }
   }
   ```

4. Test the Grails Setup by accessing this URL http://localhost:8080/myfirstapp/.

   ```
   cd myfirstapp
   ```

5. Download the security jars for Grails.

```
grails install-plugin spring-security-core
grails  s2-quickstart org.packt SecuredUser SecuredRole
```

If the installer is not supported in your version of Grails you can add a dependency to BuildConfig.groovy file:

```
plugins {

    compile ':spring-security-core:2.0-RC2'

}
```

6. Update the Bootstrap.groovy file:

```
import org.packt.SecuredUser;
import org.packt.SecuredRole;
import org.packt.SecuredUserSecuredRole
class BootStrap {

  def springSecurityService

    def init = { servletContext ->

    if(!SecuredUser.count()){
      /*The default password is 'password'*/
      def password = 'password'
      def user = new SecuredUser(username : 'anjana',
        password:'anjana123',enabled:true,
          accountExpired : false , accountLocked : false
            ,passwordExpired : false).save(flush:
              true, insert: true)
      def role = new SecuredUser(authority :
        'ROLE_USER').save(flush: true, insert: true)
      /*create the first user role map*/
      SecuredUserSecuredRole.create user , role , true
    }

    }
    def destroy = {
    }
}
```

In the preceding file we have populated users with username as anjana and password as anjana123.

Just by doing this we can authenticate the user.

You can see that we have not updated any XML file. We have just installed the plugin and have modified the file.

How it works...

Let's see what kind of output we get when we run Grails: `grails run-app`.

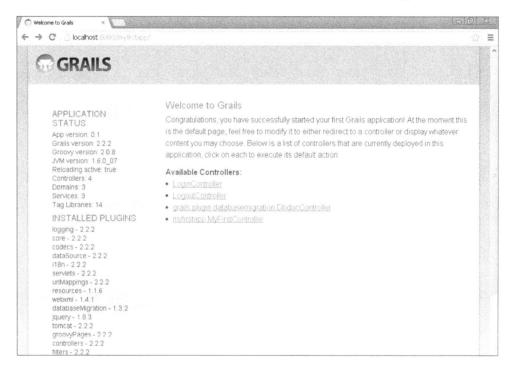

Update the `Messages.properties` file in the `i18n` folder:

```
springSecurity.login.header=Spring Security login
springSecurity.login.username.label=UserName
springSecurity.login.password.label=Password
springSecurity.login.remember.me.label=remember me
springSecurity.login.button=Login
springSecurity.errors.login.fail=Authentication failed
```

Click on the **LoginController** link at `http://localhost:8080/myfirstapp/login/auth`.

You should be able to see the login screen which is generated by the Grails framework when we installed the security plugin. The pages are available in the views folder. Now you can login with the username and password: `anjana, anjana123`. You will be redirected to the Grails home page. On failure of authentication you will get an authentication failure message.

When you click on the **LogoutController** link, you will be logged out. When you again click on the controller you will be asked to log in again.

Below is the workflow of the application:

This is the Grails login screen—on the clicking on **Login** button, after entering the username and password, this submits the credentials to the Spring Security framework:

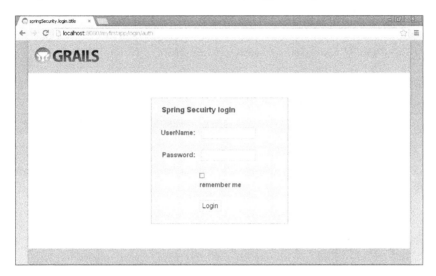

On failure of authentication, the user is redirected to the login screen with **Authentication failed** message.

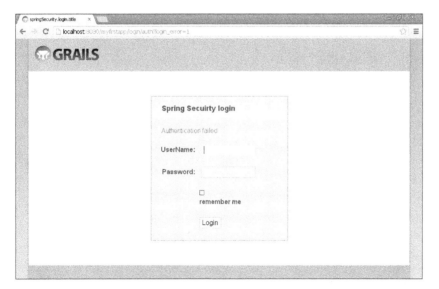

See also

- The *Spring Security with Grails to Secure Grails controller* recipe
- The *Spring Security with Groovy Grails logout scenario* recipe
- The *Spring Security with Groovy Grails Basic authentication* recipe
- The *Spring Security with Groovy Grails Digest authentication* recipe
- The *Spring Security with Groovy Grails multilevel authentication* recipe
- The *Spring Security with Groovy Grails LDAP authentication* recipe

Spring Security with Grails to secure Grails controller

Let's apply Spring Security to Grails controller. The scenario is that the user will access the Grails application and will be provided with a link to log in. On successful authentication, the user will be provided with links which he can access. The links are visible only to the logged in user.

Getting ready

For demonstration purposes we will create the following:

- A simple Grails controller: `myfirstapp`
- A `MyFirstController` controller which will be secured with Spring Security
- Modify `index.gsp`

How to do it...

The following steps are taken for integrating Spring Security with Grails to secure Grails Controller:

1. Go to `myfirstapp\grails-app\views`.
2. You will see the `index.gsp` file, rename it to `index.gsp_backup`. I have copied the styles from `index.gsp_backup`.
3. Create a new `index.gsp` file, edit the file as shown:

```
<!DOCTYPE html>
<html>
  <head>
  </head>
  <body>
```

```
<h1>Welcome to Grails</h1>
<sec:ifLoggedIn>
  Access the
    <g:link controller='myFirst' action=''>Secured
      Controller</g:link><br/>
    <g:link controller='logout' action=''>Spring
      Logout</g:link>
</sec:ifLoggedIn>

<sec:ifNotLoggedIn>
<h2>You are seeing a common page.You can click on
  login.After login success you will be provided with
    the links which you can access.</h2>
<g:link controller='login' action='auth'>Spring
  Login</g:link>
</sec:ifNotLoggedIn>

  </body>
</html>
```

How it works...

Access the URL: `http://localhost:8080/myfirstapp/`.

Now click on the **Spring Login** link, you will be redirected to a login page. Spring Security handles the authentication mechanism, where on successful login, the user will be provided with a link to access the secured controller.

The links are provided in the `index.gsp` page which will show and hide links based on the logged in or logged out status. This is provided using the security tags in the `index.gsp` pages.

Click on the link **Secured Controller**. You should be able to see the output message of the secured controller on the browser.

See also

- The *Spring Security with Groovy Grails logout scenario* recipe
- The *Spring Security with Groovy Grails Basic authentication* recipe
- The *Spring Security with Groovy Grails Digest authentication* recipe
- The *Spring Security with Groovy Grails multilevel authentication* recipe
- The *Spring Security with Groovy Grails LDAP authentication* recipe

Spring Security authentication with Groovy Grails logout scenario

In this recipe, let's look at the logout implementation with Spring Security in the Grails application.

Getting ready

When we install the Spring Security plugin with Grails, the `Login Controller` and `Logout Controller` class will be created automatically. `Login Controller` will handle the authentication. The `Logout Controller` will handle the logout process, it will redirect the user to the common page.

How to do it...

The following steps are taken to implement the logout action in the Groovy on Grails application:

1. In the `index.jsp` file we add the following:

   ```
   <g:link controller='logout' action=''>Spring
     Logout</g:link>
   ```

2. The `Logout Controller` class to redirect the request to `j_spring_security`:

   ```
   import
     org.codehaus.groovy.grails.plugins.
       springsecurity.SpringSecurityUtils

   class LogoutController {

     /**
      * Index action. Redirects to the Spring security logout uri.
      */
     def index = {
       // TODO put any pre-logout code here
       redirect uri:
         SpringSecurityUtils.securityConfig.logout.
           filterProcessesUrl // '/j_spring_security_logout'
     }
   }
   ```

How it works...

Click on the logout link. The user is redirected the home page. `SpringSecurityUtils.securityConfig.logout.filterProcessesUrl` is set to `/j_spring_security_logout` by default. So when the user clicks on logout, they are redirected to `/j_spring_security_logout action`. This will logout the user from the accessible page and the user has to again login to the Grails application.

See also

- ▶ The *Spring Security with Groovy Grails Basic authentication* recipe
- ▶ The *Spring Security with Groovy Grails Digest authentication* recipe
- ▶ The *Spring Security with Groovy Grails multilevel authentication* recipe
- ▶ The *Spring Security with Groovy Grails LDAP authentication* recipe

Spring Security with Groovy Grails Basic authentication

In this recipe, we shall demonstrate Security with Groovy on Grails using the Basic authentication mechanism.

Getting ready

- We need to create a Grails application: `grailsbasicauthexample`
- Install the Spring Security plugin to the new application
- Create `User` and `Role` classes
- Edit the `Config.groovy` file
- Edit `BootStrap.groovy` file
- Create a controller: `GreetingsController`

How to do it...

The following steps are taken for demonstrating Basic authentication with Groovy on Grails using Spring Security:

1. Run the following commands in the command prompt:
   - `Grails create-app grailsbasicauthexample`
   - `cd grailsbasicauthexample`
   - `grails install-plugin spring-security-core`
   - `grails s2-quickstart com.packt SecuredUser SecuredRole`

2. Edit the `config.groovy` file and set the following values:
   ```
   grails.plugins.springsecurity.useBasicAuth = true
   grails.plugins.springsecurity.basic.realmName =
     "HTTP Basic Auth Demo"
   ```

3. Edit the `Bootstrap.groovy` file:
   ```
   import com.packt.*;
   class BootStrap {
     def init = { servletContext ->
       def userRole =
         SecuredRole.findByAuthority("ROLE_USER") ?:
           new SecuredRole(authority: "ROLE_USER").
             save(flush: true)
       def user = SecuredUser.findByUsername("anjana") ?:
         new SecuredUser(username: "anjana", password:
   ```

```
         "anjana123", enabled: true).save(flush: true)
      SecuredUserSecuredRole.create(user, userRole, true)
   }
   def destroy = {
   }
}
```

4. Run the command `$grails create-controller Greetings` and add annotations:

```
package grailsbasicauthexample
import grails.plugins.springsecurity.Secured
class GreetingsController {
  @Secured(['ROLE_USER'])
  def index() {
    render "Hello PACKT"
  }
}
```

How it works...

Access the URL: `http://localhost:8080/grailsbasicauthexample/`.

Click on the **Greetings Controller** link. This is a secured link which has been restricted using Spring Security. When the user clicks on the link, the Basic authentication mechanism triggers a login dialog box to be filled. The user has to enter username/password: `anjana`/`anjana123`, then on authentication, the user gets redirected to an authorized page, that is, you will be prompted with the **Greetings Controller** link.

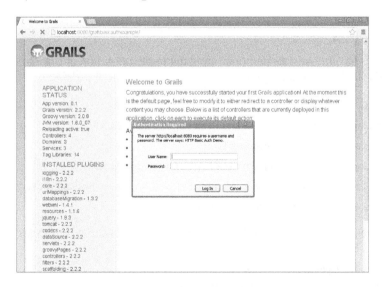

On successful authentication, the user is provided access to the greetings controller.

See also

- ▸ The *Spring Security with Groovy Grails Digest authentication* recipe
- ▸ The *Spring Security with Groovy Grails multilevel authentication* recipe
- ▸ The *Spring Security with Groovy Grails LDAP authentication* recipe

Spring Security with Groovy Grails Digest authentication

In this recipe, let's look at the Digest authentication mechanism in which the password will be hashed. Let's integrate this with the Grails application and see how it does authentication and authorization with it.

Getting ready

- ▸ We need to create a Grails application: `grailsdigestauthexample`
- ▸ Install Spring Security plugin to the new application
- ▸ Create `User` and `Role` classes
- ▸ Edit the `Config.groovy` file
- ▸ Edit the `BootStrap.groovy` file
- ▸ Create a controller: `SecuredPackt`

How to do it...

The following steps are taken for demonstrating the implementation of Digest authentication with Groovy on Grails using Spring Security:

1. In the command prompt run the following commands:

   ```
   $grails create-app grailsdigestauthexample
   $cd grailsdigestauthexample
   $grails install-plug-in spring-security-core
   $grails s2-quickstart com.packt SecuredUser SecuredRole
   $grails create-controller SecuredPackt
   ```

2. Add the following to the `config.groovy` file and edit the `Bootstrap.groovy` file:

   ```
   import com.packt.*;
   class BootStrap {
     def init = { servletContext ->
   ```

```
      def userRole = SecuredRole.findByAuthority("ROLE_USER")
        ?: new SecuredRole(authority:
          "ROLE_USER").save(flush: true)
      def user = SecuredUser.findByUsername("anjana") ?:
        new SecuredUser(username: "anjana", password:
          "anjana123", enabled: true).save(flush: true)
      SecuredUserSecuredRole.create(user, userRole, true)
    }
    def destroy = {
    }
  }
```

3. Edit the `SecuredPacktController` file and add the annotations:

```
package grailsdigestauthexample
import grails.plugins.springsecurity.Secured
class SecuredPacktController {
  @Secured(['ROLE_USER'])
  def index() {
  render "Hello PACKT"
  }
}
```

Grails with Spring Security plugin requires a username to be passed as a salt value.

We need to do a little tweaking with the generated `SecuredUser.groovy` file.

4. Update the `SecuredUser.groovy` file, as shown in the following code:

```
package com.packt
class SecuredUser {
  transient passwordEncoder

  String username
  String password
  boolean enabled
  boolean accountExpired
  boolean accountLocked
  boolean passwordExpired

  static constraints = {
    username blank: false, unique: true
    password blank: false
  }

  static mapping = {
    password column: '`password`'
  }
```

```
Set<SecuredRole> getAuthorities() {
  SecuredUserSecuredRole.findAllBySecuredUser(this).
    collect { it.securedRole } as Set
}

def beforeInsert() {
  encodePassword()
}

def beforeUpdate() {
  if (isDirty('password')) {
    encodePassword()
  }
}

protected void encodePassword() {
  password = passwordEncoder.encodePassword(password,
    username)
}
}
```

Display the logged in user:

```
<!DOCTYPE html>
<html>
  <head>
    <meta name="layout" content="main"/>
    <title>Welcome to Grails</title>

  </head>
  <body>

    <div id="page-body" role="main">
      <h1>Welcome to Grails</h1>


        <sec:ifLoggedIn>
        Hello <sec:username/>
        Access the
        <g:link controller='securedPackt' action=''>
          Secured Controller</g:link><br/>
        <g:link controller='logout' action=''>Spring
          Logout</g:link>
        </sec:ifLoggedIn>
```

```
<sec:ifNotLoggedIn>
    <h2>You are seeing a common page.You can click
        on login. After login success you will be
            provided with the links which you can
                access.</h2>
    <g:link controller='securedPackt' action=''>
        Secured Controller</g:link><br/>

</sec:ifNotLoggedIn>
    </div>
    </div>
    </body>
</html>
```

How it works...

When the user accesses the URL `http://localhost:8080/grailsdigestauthexample/`, Spring Security will prompt the user with a login dialog box asking for the username and password. When the user enters the username and password, Spring Security authenticates it and redirects the user to the secured page.

The work flow of the application is as follows:

`http://localhost:8080/grailsdigestauthexample/`

The following screenshot depicts the login dialog box that pops up when trying to access the secured resource:

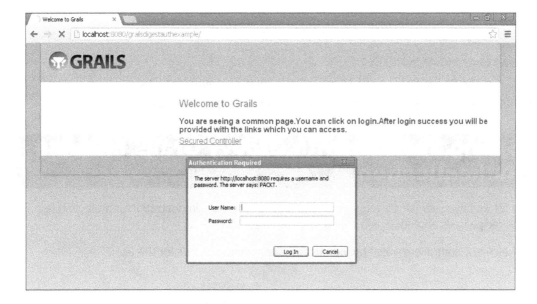

It works in a similar way to Basic authentication.

On successful login, you will get a logout link. The user has now got access to the secured controller:

Displaying the logged in user:

See also

▶ The *Spring Security with Groovy Grails multilevel authentication* recipe
▶ The *Spring Security with Groovy Grails LDAP authentication* recipe

Spring Security with Groovy Grails multiple authentication

So far we have seen single-role authentication. Let's see a demonstration of multiple roles. The recipe uses another plugin called `spring-security-ui`.

It has many controllers which provide user management screens for the user.

This saves developer time in coding these screens. It also provides a search option with autocomplete.

The `spring-security-ui` plugin also requires additional plugins to be installed which will be prompted at the console. There is an alternative to installing the plugin, that is, you can give the dependency directly in the `BuildConfig.groovy` file.

```
grails.project.dependency.resolution = {
  ...
  plugins {
    compile ":spring-security-ui:0.2""
  }
}
```

Getting ready

We need to do the following for achieving a multilevel authentication:

- ▸ Create a Grails app
- ▸ Install the `spring-security-core` plugin
- ▸ Install the `spring-security-ui` plugin
- ▸ Use the `quickstart` command to create the `Role` and `User` domain classes
- ▸ Create the `Sample` controller
- ▸ Edit the `BootStrap.groovy` file
- ▸ Edit the `SampleController` class for roles
- ▸ Update the `.gsp` files

How to do it...

The following steps are taken for implementing multiple authentication with Groovy on Grails and Spring Security:

1. Go to the Grails workspace and run the following commands:

   - ❏ grails create-app multilevelroledemo
   - ❏ cd multilevelroledemo
   - ❏ grails install-plugin spring-security-core
   - ❏ grails install-plugin spring-security-ui
   - ❏ grails s2-quickstart com.packt.security SecuredUser SecuredRole
   - ❏ grails create-controller Sample

2. Edit the `SampleController` file:

```
package multilevelroledemo
import grails.plugins.springsecurity.Secured
class SampleController {

  def index = {}

  @Secured(['ROLE_USER'])
  def user = {
    render 'Secured for ROLE_USER'
  }

  @Secured(['ROLE_ADMIN'])
  def admin = {
    render 'Secured for ROLE_ADMIN'
  }

  @Secured(['ROLE_SUPERADMIN'])
  def superadmin = {
    render 'Secured for ROLE_SUPERADMIN'
  }
}
```

3. Edit the `BootStrap.groovy` file. I have added multiple roles. These roles and users will be created from the domain groovy files that are generated:

```
import com.packt.security.SecuredRole
import com.packt.security.SecuredUser
import com.packt.security.SecuredUserSecuredRole
class BootStrap {
  def init = { servletContext ->
    def userRole =
      SecuredRole.findByAuthority("ROLE_USER") ?: new
        SecuredRole(authority: "ROLE_USER").save(flush:
          true)
    def user = SecuredUser.findByUsername("anjana") ?: new
      SecuredUser(username: "anjana", password:
        "anjana123", enabled: true).save(flush: true)
    SecuredUserSecuredRole.create(user, userRole, true)

    def userRole_admin = SecuredRole.findByAuthority
      ("ROLE_ADMIN") ?: new SecuredRole(authority:
        "ROLE_ADMIN").save(flush: true)
    def user_admin = SecuredUser.findByUsername("raghu") ?:
      new SecuredUser(username: "raghu", password:
        "raghu123", enabled: true).save(flush: true)
```

```
    SecuredUserSecuredRole.create(user_admin,
      userRole_admin, true)

    def userRole_superadmin = SecuredRole.findByAuthority
      ("ROLE_SUPERADMIN") ?: new SecuredRole(authority:
        "ROLE_SUPERADMIN").save(flush: true)
    def user_superadmin = SecuredUser.findByUsername
      ("packt") ?: new SecuredUser(username: "packt",
        password: "packt123", enabled: true).save(flush:
          true)
    SecuredUserSecuredRole.create(user_superadmin,
      userRole_superadmin, true)
  }
  def destroy = {
  }
}
```

4. Modify the `.gsp` files. Add an `index.gsp` file inside `views/sample`:

```
<head>
  <meta name='layout' content='main' />
  <title>Multi level  Roles in Grails</title>
</head>

<body>
  <div class='nav'>
    <span class='menuButton'><a class='home' href='${createLinkTo(
dir:'')}'>Home</a></span>
  </div>
  <div class='body'>
    <g:link action='user'> ROLE_USER</g:link><br/>
    <g:link action='admin'>ROLE_ADMIN</g:link><br/>
    <g: link action='superadmin'>
      ROLE_SUPERADMIN</g:link><br/>
  </div>
</body>
```

5. Add the `SecurityConfig.groovy` file inside the `config` folder:

```
security {
  active = true
  loginUserDomainClass = 'com.packt.security.SecuredUser'
  authorityDomainClass = 'com.packt.security.SecuredPackt'
  useRequestMapDomainClass = false
  useControllerAnnotations = true
}
```

How it works...

Let's see how it works. Also we get to see the controllers provided by `spring-security-ui` and its functions.

We have three users here with different roles. They are created in the `Bootstrap.groovy` file using the domain classes:

- `anjana/anjana123` as ROLE_USER
- `raghu/raghu123` as ROLE_ADMIN
- `packt/packt123` as ROLE_SUPERADMIN

Access the URL: `http://localhost:8080/multilevelroledemo/`.

You will see the Grails home page with the list of controllers.

Click on the **spring.security.ui.usercontroller** link. This controller belongs to the `spring-security-ui` plugin. This controller provides a user management screen. This controller provides the search functionality for the user. It's a wonderful UI, it has even got an autocomplete option with search filters. You can go to the link:

`http://localhost:8080/multilevelroledemo/user/search`

The following screenshot shows the Spring user management console where you can see an option to search users:

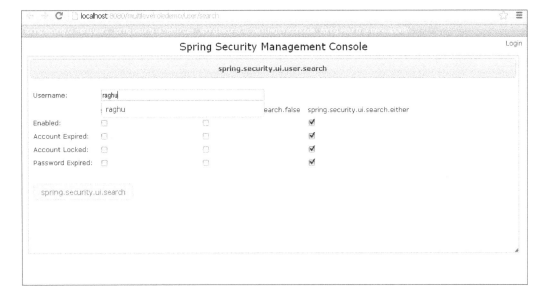

Let's look at the search result, as shown in the following screenshot:

Let's now check the role controller provided in the `spring-security-ui` plugin. This controller gives an option to search for roles and also provides roles with user mapping. It provides an option to update the roles as well:

`http://localhost:8080/multilevelroledemo/role/roleSearch`

You can also create a user, the option is available with menus. Access the following link to create a user:

`http://localhost:8080/multilevelroledemo/user/create`

Let's look at the sample controller that we have created for the application:

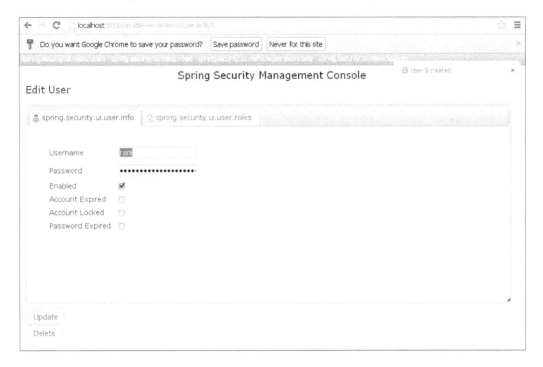

The following URL shows the sample controller mappings with various roles. This is also provided with the `spring-security-ui` plugin:

`http://localhost:8080/multilevelroledemo/securityInfo/mappings`

Let's access the sample controller at `http://localhost:8080/multilevelroledemo/sample/index`.

It displays the three roles. Click on the links and you will be prompted to log in.

Log in with the appropriate username and password, and your role information will be displayed.

The `spring-security-ui` plugin itself provides an option to log in and log out which is applicable throughout the application.

We can only use annotations, that is, `@Secured` annotations to authenticate and authorize the user for certain actions.

We can also omit the creation of users in `Bootstrap.groovy`.

See also

▸ The *Spring Security with Groovy Grails LDAP authentication* recipe

Spring Security with Groovy Grails LDAP authentication

Let's further explore the `spring-security` plugin with Groovy on Grails with LDAP authentication. In this recipe, I have used **Apache DS** with Apache Studio installed on my machine. I would be using this for authentication.

Burt Beckwith has written very nice blogs on it. You can view them at: `http://burtbeckwith.com/blog/`

Getting ready

▸ Create a Grails app: `grailssecurityldapexamplex`.

▸ Let's create a controller: `SampleController`.

▸ Install the following plugins:

  ❑ `spring-security-core`

  ❑ `spring-security-ldap`

▸ Edit the `Config.groovy` file.

▸ We shall display the role and user details after successful authentication. In this recipe we are authenticating users against the email address and password.

▸ We need to provide the Apache DS details and port number in `Config.groovy`.

▸ I am using a separate partition `sevenseas`. You can create your own domain by adding a separate `jdmpartition`.

- There are two kinds of roles: User and admin. The roles mapped with the users in Apache DS. I have created two "Organizational Units" in Apache DS:

  - **people**: This will have users

  - **groups**: This will have roles with users mapped to it

- I am getting `username`, `role`, and `email` from the Apache DS.

How to do it...

The following steps are taken for implementing `spring-security` with Grails to authenticate with LDAP:

1. Install the below commands to install plug-in:

   - `create-app  grailssecurityldapexample`

   - `cd grailssecurityldapexample`

   - `grails install-plugin spring-security-core`

   - `grails install-plugin spring-security-ldap`

   - `grails create-controller Sample`

2. Let's first update the `message.properties` file for clean UI:

   ```
   springSecurity.login.header=Spring Security login
   springSecurity.login.username.label=UserName
   springSecurity.login.password.label=Password
   springSecurity.login.remember.me.label=remember me
   springSecurity.login.button=Login
   springSecurity.errors.login.fail=Authentication failed
   ```

   Let's then configure the Apache DS properties in the `Config.groovy` file.

3. This configuration will tell Grails to authenticate the user against their e-mail ID:

   ```
   grails.plugins.springsecurity.ldap.search.filter =
     '(mail={0})'
   grails.plugins.springsecurity.ldap.context.server =
     'ldap://localhost:10389/o=sevenSeas'
   grails.plugins.springsecurity.ldap.context.managerDn =
     'uid=admin,ou=system'
   grails.plugins.springsecurity.ldap.context.managerPassword
     = 'secret'
   grails.plugins.springsecurity.ldap.authorities.
     groupSearchBase ='ou=groups'
   grails.plugins.springsecurity.ldap.authorities.
     groupSearchFilter = '(uniqueMember={0})'
   ```

```
grails.plugins.springsecurity.ldap.authorities.
  retrieveDatabaseRoles = false
grails.plugins.springsecurity.ldap.authorities.
  ignorePartialResultException= true
grails.plugins.springsecurity.ldap.search.
  base = 'ou=people'
grails.plugins.springsecurity.ldap.search.
  filter = '(mail={0})'
grails.plugins.springsecurity.ldap.search.
  attributesToReturn = ['cn', 'sn','mail']
grails.plugins.springsecurity.ldap.authenticator.
  attributesToReturn = ['cn', 'sn','mail']
```

4. Edit the controller:

```
package grailssecurityldapexample
class SampleController {
  def index() {
    render "Hello PACKT"
    }
}
```

5. Edit the `resource.groovy` file with Bean mapping.

```
beans = {
ldapUserDetailsMapper(MyUserDetailsContextMapper) {
}
}
```

6. Replace the existing `body` tag of `index,gsp` with the following code:

```
<body>
  <a href="#page-body" class="skip"><g:message
    code="default.link.skip.label" default="Skip to
      content&hellip;"/></a>

  <div id="page-body" role="main">
      <h1>Welcome to Grails</h1>
      <sec:ifLoggedIn>
Your Details<br/>
      Name:<sec:loggedInUserInfo field="fullname"/> <br/>
      Email:<sec:loggedInUserInfo field="email"/> <br/>
      Role:<sec:loggedInUserInfo field="title"/> <br/>
      <g:link controller='sample' action=''>Sample
        Controller</g:link><br/>
      (<g:link controller="logout">Logout</g:link>)
      </sec:ifLoggedIn>
      <sec:ifNotLoggedIn>
```

```html
<h2>You are seeing a common page. You can click on
  login. After login success you will be provided with
    the links which you can access.</h2>
<g:link controller='login' action='auth'>Spring
  Login</g:link>
</sec:ifNotLoggedIn>



  </div>
  </body>
```

7. Create `MyUserDetails.groovy` under `src/groovy`:

```groovy
import org.springframework.security.core.GrantedAuthority
import org.springframework.security.core.userdetails.User

class MyUserDetails extends User {
 String fullname
 String email
 String title

MyUserDetails(String username, String password, boolean
  enabled, boolean accountNonExpired, boolean
    credentialsNonExpired, boolean accountNonLocked,
      Collection authorities, String fullname,
String email, String title) {
  super(username, password, enabled, accountNonExpired,
    credentialsNonExpired, accountNonLocked, authorities)
this.fullname = fullname
this.email = email
this.title = title
}
}
```

8. Let's create a `ContextMapper` for LDAP.

    We are getting the LDAP attributes here:

```groovy
import org.springframework.ldap.core.DirContextAdapter
import org.springframework.ldap.core.DirContextOperations
import org.springframework.security.core.
  userdetails.UserDetails
import org.springframework.security.ldap.
  userdetails.UserDetailsContextMapper
class MyUserDetailsContextMapper implements
  UserDetailsContextMapper {
    UserDetails mapUserFromContext(DirContextOperations
      ctx, String username, Collection authorities) {
```

```
String fullname = ctx.originalAttrs.
  attrs['cn'].values[0]
String email = ctx.originalAttrs.attrs['mail'].
  values[0].toString().toLowerCase()
def title = ctx.originalAttrs.attrs['sn']
def userDetails = new MyUserDetails(username, '',
  true, true, true, true,
    authorities, fullname,email,  title == null ? ''
      : title.values[0])
return userDetails
    }
    void mapUserToContext(UserDetails user,
      DirContextAdapter ctx) {
        throw new IllegalStateException("Only retrieving
          data from LDAP is currently supported")
    }

}
```

Execute the following command for the app:

`grails run-app`

How it works...

When the user accesses the URL: `http://localhost:8080/`
`grailssecurityldapexample/`, they will see a common page with a link. In the login
form enter the username and password. Clicking on **submit**, the Grails will submit the URL to
Spring Security. Spring Security connects with the LDAP details provided and queries the LDAP
with the username. On success, the user is directed to the success URL.

Access the URL: `http://localhost:8080/grailssecurityldapexample/`.

Click on the **Spring Login** link and enter the username: `admin@test.com` and password: `123456`.

Click on **Logout**.

Click on **Spring Login** link and enter the username: `test@test.com` and password: `pass`. The Grails application submits the credentials to the Spring Security framework which queries the LDAP and retrieves the user details and displays it on the secured page:

See also

▶ *Chapter 6, Spring Security with Vaadin*

▶ *Chapter 5, Spring Security with GWT*

5
Spring Security with GWT

In this chapter we will cover:

- Spring Security with GWT authentication using Spring Security Beans
- Form-based authentication with GWT and Spring Security
- Basic authentication with GWT and Spring Security
- Digest authentication with GWT and Spring Security
- Database authentication with GWT and Spring Security
- LDAP authentication with GWT and Spring Security

Introduction

Google web development tool kit (GWT) provides a standard framework for developing java web applications. GWT was developed to create rich Internet applications and will be a good option if you want to go for cross-browser compatibility. Modern browsers, for example, Mozilla and Chrome, provide GWT plugins which can be installed on all browsers. There are various plugins available for different IDEs including Eclipse, NetBeans, and many others. These plugins have increased the speed of development. The GWT plugin for Eclipse comes with an internal Jetty server on which applications are automatically deployed. GWT also reduces dependency on javascript developers since the GWT code is converted into all browser compatible javascript and HTML by the GWT compiler which comes with the GWT-SDK.

In this chapter we will demonstrate Spring Security with GWT integration using various approaches. Let's first do a basic setup for it. It's all about downloading the plugin and creating a sample GWT project.

Spring Security with GWT authentication using Spring Security Beans

So far in all our previous demonstrations we have been giving the configurations in the `applicationContext.xml` file. In the following recipe we will take a different approach. In this approach we will see how we can use the authentication provider interface and the authentication interface available in the Spring Security API to do the authentication.

GWT plugin by default will create a greetings application which will greet the user by accepting the user name. Our goal is to apply security on top of this. We would like to prompt the user with Spring Security login page on startup and then take the user into the application.

Getting ready

- Download Eclipse Indigo from: `http://dl.google.com/eclipse/plugin/3.7`.
- If you are using a different one go for: `https://developers.google.com/eclipse/docs/download`.
- Create a GWT web project in Eclipse—this will generate a default GWT application that will greet the user.
- In any GWT application you can see the following modules:
  - **Configuration module**: This will have the `gwt.xml` file
  - **Client**: This will have two interfaces-async interface and another interface that extends *RemoteService* interface
  - **Server**: Will have the `Implementation` class which implements the client interface and extends the remote Service Servlet
  - **Shared**: This will have classes to check for data validation
  - **Test**: You can add your junit test cases here
  - **War**: This will have the `web-inf` folder
- Run the application on the internal server. You will get a URL.
- Open the URL in the Mozilla Firefox browser; you will get a prompt to download the GWT plugin and install it.
- You will be prompted to input a user name and, when entered, you will get a dialog box which will give the user details.
- Our aim is to apply security on startup of the application, that is, we would like to identify the user who is accessing the GWT application.
- Create an `applicationContext.xml` file. It's mandatory to name it as `applicationContext` or else we will get error messages in the console.
- Edit the `web.xml` file with spring listeners.

▶ Make sure the `war/web-inf/lib` folder has the following JAR files:

  ❏ `gwt-servlet`

  ❏ `spring-security-config-3.1.4.Release`

  ❏ `spring-security-core-3.1.4.Release`

  ❏ `spring-security-web-3.1.4.Release`

  ❏ `org.spring-framework.core-3.1.4.Release`

  ❏ `org.spring-framework.context.support-3.1.4.Release`

  ❏ `org.springframework.context-3.1.4.Release`

  ❏ `org.springframework.expression-3.1.4.Release`

  ❏ `org.springframework.aop-3.1.4.Release`

  ❏ `org.springframework.aspects-3.1.4.Release`

  ❏ `org.springframework.asm-3.1.4.Release`

  ❏ `org.springframework.web-3.1.4.Release`

  ❏ `org.springframework.web.servelet-3.1.4.Release`

  ❏ `org.springframework.instrument-3.1.4.Release`

  ❏ `org.springframework.instrument-tomcat-3.1.4.Release`

How to do it...

1. Update the `Web.xml` file with Spring Listener and Spring Filter:

```
<filter>
  <filter-name>springSecurityFilterChain</filter-name>
  <filter-class>org.springframework.web.filter.
    DelegatingFilterProxy</filter-class>
</filter>

<filter-mapping>
  <filter-name>springSecurityFilterChain</filter-name>
  <url-pattern>/*</url-pattern>
</filter-mapping>

<listener>
  <listener-class>
  org.springframework.web.context.ContextLoaderListener
  </listener-class>
</listener>
```

You can observe that we haven't configured the `<context-param>` as in our previous applications. Spring will automatically look out for the `applicationContext.xml` file.

2. Edit the `applicationContext.xml` file:

```xml
<http auto-config="true">
  <intercept-url pattern="/xyz/**" access="ROLE_AUTHOR"/>
  <intercept-url pattern="/xyz/**" access="ROLE_AUTHOR"/>
  <intercept-url pattern="/**/*.html" access="ROLE_AUTHOR"/>
  <intercept-url pattern="/**"
    access="IS_AUTHENTICATED_ANONYMOUSLY" />
</http>
<beans:bean id="packtAuthenticationListener"
  class="com.demo.xyz.server.PacktAuthenticationListener"/>
<beans:bean id="packtGWTAuthenticator"
  class="com.demo.xyz.server.PacktGWTAuthenticator" />
<authentication-manager alias="authenticationManager">
  <authentication-provider ref="packtGWTAuthenticator"/>
</authentication-manager>
</beans:beans>
```

This configuration will also give hints to the next steps. You can observe that we have not configured any `<login-page>` or its URL. We have only given URLs that need security. The `<authentication-provider>` is mapped with a custom class.

We have also configured two Beans that are the listener and authenticator.

Spring's context API allows us to create listeners to track events in the application. If you recall, we had also used listeners phase listener in our JSF application to track the security-related events and errors.

The `PacktGWTAuthenticator` implements the authentication provider interfaces.

3. Create an authenticator using the Spring authentication provider:

```java
Package com.demo.xyz.server
public class PacktGWTAuthenticator implements
AuthenticationProvider{
  static Users users=new Users();
  private static Map<String, String> usersMap =users.loadUsers();

  @Override
  public Authentication authenticate
    (Authentication authentication)
  throws AuthenticationException {

    String mylogin_name = (String) authentication.getPrincipal();
    String mypassword = (String)authentication.getCredentials();
    //check username
```

```
      if (usersMap.get(mylogin_name)==null)
      throw new UsernameNotFoundException
        (mylogin_name+"credential not found in the UsersMap");
//get password
      String password = usersMap.get(mylogin_name);

      if (!password.equals(mypassword))
        throw new BadCredentialsException("Incorrect password-
          or credential not found in the UsersMap");

      Authentication packtauthenticator =  new
        PacktGWTAuthentication("ROLE_AUTHOR", authentication);
      packtauthenticator .setAuthenticated(true);

      return packtauthenticator;

    }

    @Override
    public boolean supports(Class<? extends Object>
        authentication) {
    return UsernamePasswordAuthenticationToken.class
      .isAssignableFrom(authentication);
    }
}
```

Here, `authenticate ()` and `supports ()` are the authentication provider-interface methods. The User class will load the users.

4. Create a `User` class to load the users:

```
package com.demo.xyz.server;
import java.util.HashMap;
import java.util.Map;
public class Users {
  public Map<String, String> getUsersMap() {
    return usersMap;
  }

  public void setUsersMap(Map<String, String> usersMap) {

    this.usersMap = usersMap;
  }

  private Map<String, String> usersMap = new HashMap
    <String, String>();
```

```
      public Map<String, String> loadUsers(){
        usersMap.put("rashmi", "rashmi123");
        usersMap.put("shami", "shami123");
        usersMap.put("ravi", "ravi123");
        usersMap.put("ratty", "ratty123");
        return usersMap;
      }

    }
```

The above class has few getters and setters. And a method to load users.

5. Implementing the Spring authentication class to get the user information:

```
public class PacktGWTAuthentication implements
  Authentication{

  private static final long serialVersionUID =
    -3091441742758356129L;

  private boolean authenticated;

  private GrantedAuthority grantedAuthority;
  private Authentication authentication;


  public PacktGWTAuthentication(String role,
    Authentication authentication) {
    this.grantedAuthority = new GrantedAuthorityImpl(role);
    this.authentication = authentication;
  }

  @Override
  public Object getCredentials() {
    return authentication.getCredentials();
  }

  @Override
  public Object getDetails() {
    return authentication.getDetails();
  }

  @Override
  public Object getPrincipal() {
    return authentication.getPrincipal();
  }
```

```
@Override
public boolean isAuthenticated() {
  return authenticated;
}

@Override
public void setAuthenticated(boolean authenticated)
    throws IllegalArgumentException {
  this.authenticated = authenticated;
}

@Override
public String getName() {
  return this.getClass().getSimpleName();
}
@Override
public Collection<GrantedAuthority> getAuthorities() {
  Collection<GrantedAuthority> authorities =
    new ArrayList<GrantedAuthority>();
  authorities.add(granted Authority);
  return authorities;
}

}
```

Authentication interface handles the user details, principal, and credentials. The authentication provider uses this class to pass the role information.

6. Implement the interfaces declared in the GWT client package:

```
package com.demo.xyz.server;
public class PacktAuthenticatorServiceImpl extends
  RemoteServiceServlet  implements PacktAuthenticatorService
  {

  @Override
  public String authenticateServer() {
  Authentication authentication =SecurityContextHolder.
    getContext().getAuthentication();
  if (authentication==null){
    System.out.println("looks like you have not
      logged in.");
    return null;
  }
  else {
    System.out.println
```

```
        (authentication.getPrincipal().toString());
    System.out.println
        (authentication.getName().toString());
    System.out.println
        (authentication.getDetails().toString());
    return (String) authentication.getPrincipal();
    }

  }

}
```

The `authenticate Server` method implementation is found in this class. This will print the debug statements to check whether the user has logged in or not. If logged in, then we will have to get the principal and user details.

7. Use the Spring listeners to track events:

```
package com.demo.xyz.server;
public class PacktAuthenticationListener implements
  ApplicationListener<AbstractAuthenticationEvent>{
  @Override
  public void onApplicationEvent
    (AbstractAuthenticationEvent event) {

    final StringBuilder mybuilder = new StringBuilder();
    mybuilder.append("AN AUHTHENTICATION EVENT ");
    mybuilder.append(event.getClass().getSimpleName());
    mybuilder.append("*** ");
    mybuilder.append(event.getAuthentication().getName());
    mybuilder.append("$$$DETAILS OF THE EVENT: ");
    mybuilder.append(event.getAuthentication().getDetails());

    if (event instanceof
      AbstractAuthenticationFailureEvent) {
      mybuilder.append("$$$ EXCEPTION HAS OCCURED: ");
      mybuilder.append(((AbstractAuthenticationFailureEvent)
        event).getException().getMessage());
    }
    System.out.println(mybuilder.toString());
  }
}
```

This class implements the Springs application listener which is of the type `AbstractAuthenticationEvent`. We are capturing the authentication event and printing it out in the console; you can also use logger to track such events.

8. Update the GWT class on `ModuleLoad()`:

```java
package com.demo.xyz.client;

/**
 * Entry point classes define <code>onModuleLoad()</code>.
 */
public class Xyz implements EntryPoint {
/**
 * The message displayed to the user when the server cannot be
reached or
 * returns an error.
 */
private static final String SERVER_ERROR =
  "An error occurred while "+ "attempting to contact
   the server. Please check your network "
  + "connection and try again.";

/**
 * Create a remote service proxy to talk to the server-side
Greeting service.
 */
private final GreetingServiceAsync greetingService =
  GWT.create(GreetingService.class);
private final PacktAuthenticatorServiceAsync
  packtAuthenticatorService =
  GWT.create(PacktAuthenticatorService.class);
/**
 * This is the entry point method.
 */
public void onModuleLoad() {
  final Button sendButton = new Button("Send");
  final TextBox nameField = new TextBox();
  nameField.setText("GWT User");
  final Label errorLabel = new Label();
  sendButton.addStyleName("sendButton");
  RootPanel.get("nameFieldContainer").add(nameField);
  RootPanel.get("sendButtonContainer").add(sendButton);
  RootPanel.get("errorLabelContainer").add(errorLabel);

// Focus the cursor on the name field when the app loads
  nameField.setFocus(true);
  nameField.selectAll();

  // Create the popup dialog box
```

```
      final DialogBox dialogBox = new DialogBox();
      dialogBox.setText("Remote Procedure Call");
      dialogBox.setAnimationEnabled(true);
      final Button closeButton = new Button("Close");
   // We can set the id of a widget by accessing its Element
      closeButton.getElement().setId("closeButton");
      final Label textToServerLabel = new Label();
      final HTML serverResponseLabel = new HTML();
      VerticalPanel dialogVPanel = new VerticalPanel();
      dialogVPanel.addStyleName("dialogVPanel");
      dialogVPanel.add(new HTML
        ("<b>Sending name to the server:</b>"));
      dialogVPanel.add(textToServerLabel);
      dialogVPanel.add(new HTML("<br><b>Server replies:</b>"));
      dialogVPanel.add(serverResponseLabel);
      dialogVPanel.setHorizontalAlignment
        (VerticalPanel.ALIGN_RIGHT);
dialogVPanel.add(closeButton);
dialogBox.setWidget(dialogVPanel);

      // Add a handler to close the DialogBox
      closeButton.addClickHandler(new ClickHandler() {
        public void onClick(ClickEvent event) {
          dialogBox.hide();
          sendButton.setEnabled(true);
          sendButton.setFocus(true);
        }
      });

      // Create a handler for the sendButton and nameField
      class MyHandler implements ClickHandler, KeyUpHandler {

      public void onClick(ClickEvent event) {
        sendNameToServer();
      }

      public void onKeyUp(KeyUpEvent event) {
        if (event.getNativeKeyCode() == KeyCodes.KEY_ENTER) {
          sendNameToServer();
        }
      }

      /**
       * Send the name from the nameField to the server and wait for a
```

```
response.
   */
  private void sendNameToServer() {
  // First, we validate the input.
  errorLabel.setText("");
  String textToServer = nameField.getText();
  if (!FieldVerifier.isValidName(textToServer)) {
    errorLabel.setText("Please enter at least four
      characters");
    return;
    }

// Then, we send the input to the server.
    sendButton.setEnabled(false);
    textToServerLabel.setText(textToServer);
    serverResponseLabel.setText("");
    greetingService.greetServer(textToServer,
    new AsyncCallback<String>() {
      public void onFailure(Throwable caught) {
        // Show the RPC error message to the user dialogBox
        setText("Remote Procedure Call - Failure");
        serverResponseLabel.addStyleName
          ("serverResponseLabelError");
        serverResponseLabel.setHTML(SERVER_ERROR);
        dialogBox.center();
        closeButton.setFocus(true);
      }

      public void onSuccess(String result) {
        dialogBox.setText("Remote Procedure Call");
        serverResponseLabel.removeStyleName
          ("serverResponseLabelError");
        serverResponseLabel.setHTML(result);
        dialogBox.center();
        closeButton.setFocus(true);
      }
    });
  }
}

// Add a handler to send the name to the server
MyHandler handler = new MyHandler();
sendButton.addClickHandler(handler);
nameField.addKeyUpHandler(handler);
```

```
packtAuthenticatorService.authenticateServer(new
AsyncCallback<String>() {
  public void onFailure(Throwable caught) {
    dialogBox.setText("Remote Procedure Call - Failure");
  }
  public void onSuccess(String result) {
    nameField.setText(result);
  }
}
);
}
}
```

Add this code in the end of the onModuleLoad method. This is similar to registering our service on load.

9. Edit the PacktAuthenticationService class:

```
package com.demo.xyz.client;

/**
 * Entry point classes define <code>onModuleLoad()</code>.
 */
public class Xyz implements EntryPoint {
  /**
   * The message displayed to the user when the server cannot be
reached or
   * returns an error.
   */
  private static final String SERVER_ERROR =
    "An error occurred while "+ "attempting to contact
    the server. Please check your network "
    + "connection and try again.";

  /**
   * Create a remote service proxy to talk to the server-side
Greeting service.
   */
  private final GreetingServiceAsync greetingService
    = GWT.create(GreetingService.class);
  private final PacktAuthenticatorServiceAsync
    packtAuthenticatorService =
    GWT.create(PacktAuthenticatorService.class);
  /**
   * This is the entry point method.
   */
```

```java
public void onModuleLoad() {
    final Button sendButton = new Button("Send");
    final TextBox nameField = new TextBox();
    nameField.setText("GWT User");
    final Label errorLabel = new Label();

    // We can add style names to widgets
    sendButton.addStyleName("sendButton");

    // Add the nameField and sendButton to the RootPanel
    // Use RootPanel.get() to get the entire body element
    RootPanel.get("nameFieldContainer").add(nameField);
    RootPanel.get("sendButtonContainer").add(sendButton);
    RootPanel.get("errorLabelContainer").add(errorLabel);

    // Focus the cursor on the name field when the app loads
nameField.setFocus(true);
    nameField.selectAll();

    // Create the popup dialog box
    final DialogBox dialogBox = new DialogBox();
    dialogBox.setText("Remote Procedure Call");
    dialogBox.setAnimationEnabled(true);
    final Button closeButton = new Button("Close");
    //We can set the id of a widget by accessing its Element
    closeButton.getElement().setId("closeButton");
    final Label textToServerLabel = new Label();
    final HTML serverResponseLabel = new HTML();
    VerticalPanel dialogVPanel = new VerticalPanel();
    dialogVPanel.addStyleName("dialogVPanel");
    dialogVPanel.add(new HTML
        ("<b>Sending name to the server:</b>"));
    dialogVPanel.add(textToServerLabel);
    dialogVPanel.add(new HTML
        ("<br><b>Server replies:</b>"));
    dialogVPanel.add(serverResponseLabel);
    dialogVPanel.setHorizontalAlignment
        (VerticalPanel.ALIGN_RIGHT);
    dialogVPanel.add(closeButton);
    dialogBox.setWidget(dialogVPanel);

    // Add a handler to close the DialogBox
    closeButton.addClickHandler(new ClickHandler() {
        public void onClick(ClickEvent event) {
```

```
          dialogBox.hide();
          sendButton.setEnabled(true);
          sendButton.setFocus(true);
        }
      });

      // Create a handler for the sendButton and nameField
      class MyHandler implements ClickHandler, KeyUpHandler {
        /**
         * Fired when the user clicks on the sendButton.
         */
        public void onClick(ClickEvent event) {
          sendNameToServer();
        }

        /**
         * Fired when the user types in the nameField.
         */
        public void onKeyUp(KeyUpEvent event) {
          if (event.getNativeKeyCode() == KeyCodes.KEY_ENTER) {
            sendNameToServer();
          }
        }

          /**
           * Send the name from the nameField to the server and wait
  for a response.
           */
          private void sendNameToServer() {
          // First, we validate the input.
          errorLabel.setText("");
          String textToServer = nameField.getText();
          if (!FieldVerifier.isValidName(textToServer)) {
            errorLabel.setText("Please enter at least
                four characters");
            return;
          }

          // Then, we send the input to the server.
          sendButton.setEnabled(false);
          textToServerLabel.setText(textToServer);
          serverResponseLabel.setText("");
          greetingService.greetServer(textToServer,
```

```
        new AsyncCallback<String>() {
          public void onFailure(Throwable caught) {
            // Show the RPC error message to the user
            dialogBox.setText("Remote Procedure Call
              - Failure");
            serverResponseLabel.addStyleName
              ("serverResponseLabelError");
            serverResponseLabel.setHTML(SERVER_ERROR);
            dialogBox.center();
            closeButton.setFocus(true);
          }

          public void onSuccess(String result) {
          dialogBox.setText("Remote Procedure Call");
          serverResponseLabel.removeStyleName
            ("serverResponseLabelError");
          serverResponseLabel.setHTML(result);
          dialogBox.center();
          closeButton.setFocus(true);
        }
      });
    }
}


// Add a handler to send the name to the server
MyHandler handler = new MyHandler();
sendButton.addClickHandler(handler);
nameField.addKeyUpHandler(handler);
packtAuthenticatorService.authenticateServer(new
AsyncCallback<String>() {
  public void onFailure(Throwable caught) {
    dialogBox.setText("Remote Procedure Call - Failure");
}
public void onSuccess(String result) {
  nameField.setText(result);
}
}
);
}
}
```

How it works...

Now access the following URL:

`http://127.0.0.1:8888/Xyz.html?gwt.codesvr=127.0.0.1:9997`

The user will be redirected to the Spring Security internal login page. When the user enters the **User** and **Password** input and hits submit, the `PacktGWTAuthenticator` class loads the users from the `Users` class and the inputs are compared. If the map has the same credentials as the one the user has provided, authorization is initiated and, on success, the user is directed to the GWT application. The example has used Spring Security's `Authentication Provider` and `Authenticator Bean` classes explicitly by implementing the interfaces and the `application-context.xml` invokes the `PacktGWTAuthenticator` and `PacktGWTAuthentication implementation` classes to do authentication and authorization.

You will see the previous image on a successful login.

Listener generated output in the Eclipse console:

PacktGWTAuthentication

org.springframework.security.web.authentication.WebAuthenticationDetails@
fffdaa08: RemoteIpAddress: 127.0.0.1; SessionId: 1cdb5kk395o29

On a login failure the following image is displayed:

See also

> ▸ The *Form-based authentication with GWT and Spring Security* recipe
>
> ▸ The *Basic authentication with GWT and Spring Security* recipe
>
> ▸ The *Digest authentication with GWT and Spring Security* recipe
>
> ▸ The *Database authentication with GWT and Spring Security* recipe
>
> ▸ The *LDAP authentication with GWT and Spring Security* recipe

Form-based authentication with GWT and Spring Security

We will demonstrate Form-based authentication in GWT. It's very similar to the authentication that we have done in our previous recipes. We will be editing the `applicationContext.xml`.

Getting ready

► Create a sample GWT project.

► Add the spring-related JARs in the build path.

► Add the Spring Security-related JARs.

► Add the `applicationContext.xml` file.

► Edit the `web.xml` file as shown in the previous section.

► Also add the spring-related JARs in the `web-inf lib` folder.

How to do it...

Edit the `applicationContext.xml` file:

```
<http auto-config="true" >
  <intercept-url pattern="/basicgwtauth/**"
    access="ROLE_AUTHOR"/>
        <intercept-url pattern="/basicgwtauth/**" access="ROLE_
AUTHOR"/>
        <intercept-url pattern="/**/*.html" access="ROLE_AUTHOR"/>
        <intercept-url pattern="/**" access="IS_AUTHENTICATED_
ANONYMOUSLY" />

</http>
<authentication-manager>
  <authentication-provider>
    <user-service>
      <user name="anjana" password="123456"
      authorities="ROLE_AUTHOR" />
    </user-service>
  </authentication-provider>
</authentication-manager>
```

This configuration invokes the internal Spring Security login form. The idea is to show another scenario where we don't specify an authentication mechanism and spring, by default, uses its login form page to authenticate the user.

How it works...

Now access the following URL:

```
http://127.0.0.1:8888/Basicgwtauth.html?gwt.codesvr=127.0.0.1:9997
```

Enter the login username and password; you will be taken to the GWT page. This is also a mechanism to invoke spring's internal login jsp page if the developer doesn't want to create their own customized jsp. It still reads the authentication provider details provided to authenticate and authorize the user.

In a similar way you can authenticate using database and LDAP as well as just by editing the authentication manager configurations.

See also

- ▸ The *Basic authentication with GWT and Spring Security* recipe
- ▸ The *Digest authentication with GWT and Spring Security* recipe
- ▸ The *Database authentication with GWT and Spring Security* recipe
- ▸ The *LDAP authentication with GWT and Spring Security* recipe

Basic authentication with GWT and Spring Security

We will demonstrate Basic authentication in GWT. It's very similar to the basic authentication that we are going doing in later recipes. We will be editing the `applicationContext.xml`.

Getting ready

- ▸ Create a sample GWT project
- ▸ Add the spring related JARs in the build path
- ▸ Add the Spring Security related JARs
- ▸ Add the `applicationContext.xml` file
- ▸ Edit the `web.xml` file as shown in the previous section
- ▸ Also add the spring related JARs in the `web-inf lib` folder

How to do it...

Edit the `applicationContext.xml` file:

```
<http auto-config="true" >
  <intercept-url pattern="/basicgwtauth/**"
    access="ROLE_AUTHOR"/>
  <intercept-url pattern="/basicgwtauth/**"
    access="ROLE_AUTHOR"/>
  <intercept-url pattern="/**/*.html" access="ROLE_AUTHOR"/>
  <intercept-url pattern="/**"
    access="IS_AUTHENTICATED_ANONYMOUSLY" />
  <http-basic />
</http>
<authentication-manager>
  <authentication-provider>
    <user-service>
      <user name="anjana" password="123456"
        authorities="ROLE_AUTHOR" />
    </user-service>
  </authentication-provider>
</authentication-manager>
```

Here we are specifying the authentication mechanism as basic.

How it works...

Now access the URL:

```
http://127.0.0.1:8888/Basicgwtauth.html?gwt.codesvr=127.0.0.1:9997
```

Spring security will interrupt the user from accessing the GWT application. The security mechanism will be read from the `application-context.xml` file. For this application the security mechanism is basic. Spring Security will pop up a dialogue box asking for user name and password. The login username and password that the user enters will be authenticated and authorized and the user will be taken to the GWT page.

Enter the login username and password and you will be taken to the GWT page.

See also

▸ The *Digest authentication with GWT and Spring Security* recipe

▸ The *Database authentication with GWT and Spring Security* recipe

▸ The *LDAP authentication with GWT and Spring Security* recipe

Digest authentication with GWT and Spring Security

We will now demonstrate Digest authentication in GWT. It's very similar to the basic authentication that we are doing in our previous recipes. We will be editing the `applicationContext.xml`. We will be hashing the password. The setup remains the same, the only change is the `applicationcontext.xml`.

Getting ready

▸ Create a sample GWT project

▸ Add the spring-related JARs in the build path

> ▶ Add the Spring Security-related JARs

> ▶ Add the `applicationContext.xml` file

> ▶ Edit the `web.xml` file as shown in the previous section

> ▶ Also add the spring-related JARs in the `web-inf lib` folder

How to do it...

Edit the `applicationContext.xml` file:

```
<http auto-config="true" >
  <intercept-url pattern="/basicgwtauth/**" access="
    ROLE_EDITOR "/>
  <intercept-url pattern="/basicgwtauth/**" access="
    ROLE_EDITOR "/>
  <intercept-url pattern="/**/*.html" access=
    " ROLE_EDITOR "/>
  <intercept-url pattern="/**" access
    ="IS_AUTHENTICATED_ANONYMOUSLY" />
  <http-basic />
</http>
<authentication-manager>   .
  <authentication-provider>
    <password-encoder hash="sha" />
    <user-service>
      <user name="anjana"
        password="bde892ed4e131546a2f9997cc94d31e2c8f18b2a"
      authorities="ROLE_EDITOR" />
    </user-service>
  </authentication-provider>
</authentication-manager>
```

Here we are specifying the authentication mechanism as basic and have given the hashed password here. To hash the password, use the `jacksum jar`. This has already been demonstrated in *Chapter 2, Spring Security with Sturts2*.

How it works...

Now access the following URL:

```
http://127.0.0.1:8888/Basicgwtauth.html?gwt.codesvr=127.0.0.1:9997
```

The user should be redirected to the GWT application by accessing this URL. But the Spring framework interrupts this to check if the user is authorized to see the application. It pops up a login screen. Enter the login username and password and you will be taken to the GWT page.

Your password will be decoded for authentication based on the algorithm mentioned in the configuration file. The algorithm mentioned here is *Sha*. So the password will be encrypted and decrypted using *Sha algorithm*.

Enter the login username and password and you will be taken to the GWT page. Your password will be decoded for authentication based on the algorithm mentioned in the configuration file.

See also

▶ The *Database authentication with GWT and Spring Security* recipe

▶ The *LDAP authentication with GWT and Spring Security* recipe

Database authentication with GWT and Spring Security

We will demonstrate database authentication in GWT. The setup remains the same. In all our previous examples we were using `applicationContext.xml` which was easily recognized by the Spring framework since it has the default file name. In this current example we will give a new file name to this and see how the application responds. Also, we need to add the `spring-jdbc.xml`.

Getting ready

▶ Create a sample GWT project

▶ Add the spring-related JARs in the build path

▶ Add the Spring Security-related JARs

▶ Add the `spring-security.xml` file

- ▸ Add the spring-jdbc-related JARs
- ▸ Edit the `web.xml` file as shown in the previous section
- ▸ Also add the spring-related JARs in the `web-inf lib` folder

How to do it...

Edit the `spring-security.xml` file:

```
<http auto-config="true" >
  <intercept-url pattern="/springgwtdbsecurity/**"
    access="ROLE_AUTHOR"/>
  <intercept-url pattern="/springgwtdbsecurity/**"
    access="ROLE_AUTHOR"/>
  <intercept-url pattern="/**/*.html" access="ROLE_AUTHOR"/>
  <intercept-url pattern="/**"
    access="IS_AUTHENTICATED_ANONYMOUSLY" />
  <http-basic />
</http>
<authentication-manager alias="authenticationManager">
  <authentication-provider>
  <jdbc-user-service data-source-ref="dataSource"
  users-by-username-query="
  select username,password, enabled
  from users where username=?"

  authorities-by-username-query="
  select u.username, ur.authority from users u,
    user_roles ur
      where u.user_id = ur.user_id and u.username =?"/>
  </authentication-provider>
</authentication-manager>
```

Add this above in the beans tag of the `xml` file. Here we are specifying the authentication mechanism as basic and the user information is stored the database.

Edit the `spring-jdbc.xml` file:

```
<beans xmlns="http://www.springframework.org/schema/beans"
  xmlns:xsi="http://www.w3.org/2001/XMLSchema-instance"
  xsi:schemaLocation="http://www.springframework.org/
    schema/beans
  http://www.springframework.org/schema/beans/
    spring-beans-3.0.xsd">
```

```
<bean id="MySqlDatasource" class="org.springframework.
  jdbc.datasource.DriverManagerDataSource">
  <property name="driverClassName" value=
    "com.mysql.jdbc.Driver" />
  <property name="url" value=
    "jdbc:mysql://localhost:3306/packtdb" />
  <property name="username" value="root" />
<property name="password" value="packt123" />
</bean>
</beans>
```

We are giving the database information.

Edit the `web.xml` file:

```
<context-param>
  <param-name>contextConfigLocation</param-name>
  <param-value>
    /WEB-INF/spring-security.xml,
    /WEB-INF/spring-jdbc.xml
  </param-value>
</context-param>

<listener>
  <listener-class>
    org.springframework.web.context.ContextLoaderListener
  </listener-class>
</listener>
```

We have to configure the `springsecurityFilterchain`, as shown in the previous examples, and under that, add the above section.

How it works...

Now access the following URL:

```
http://127.0.0.1:8888/springgwtdbsecurity.html?gwt.
codesvr=127.0.0.1:9997
```

Enter the login username and password and you will be taken to the GWT page. A database connection will be created and a query will be executed. The user-entered values will be checked with retrieved values for authentication. With this we can see that GWT seamlessly integrates with Spring Security.

▸ The *LDAP authentication with GWT and Spring Security* recipe

LDAP authentication with GWT and Spring Security

We will demonstrate LDAP authentication in GWT. The setup remains the same: The user has to create groups and users.

Getting ready

▸ Create a sample GWT project

▸ Add the spring-related JARs in the build path

▸ Add the Spring Security-related JARs

▸ Add the `spring-security.xml` file

▸ Add the spring-LDAP-related JARs

▸ Edit the `web.xml` file as shown in the previous section

▸ Also add the spring-related JARs in the `web-inf lib` folder

How to do it...

Edit the `spring-security.xml` file:

```
<http auto-config="true" >
  <intercept-url pattern="/springgwtldapsecurity/**"
    access="ROLE_AUTHOR"/>
  <intercept-url pattern="/springgwtldapsecurity/**"
    access="ROLE_AUTHOR"/>
  <intercept-url pattern="/**/*.html" access="ROLE_AUTHOR"/>
  <intercept-url pattern="/**"
    access="IS_AUTHENTICATED_ANONYMOUSLY" />
  <http-basic />
</http>
<authentication-manager>
  <ldap-authentication-provider
    user-search-filter="(mail={0})"
    user-search-base="ou=people"
    group-search-filter="(uniqueMember={0})"
    group-search-base="ou=groups"
```

```
      group-role-attribute="cn"
      role-prefix="ROLE_">
      </ldap-authentication-provider>
   </authentication-manager>

<ldap-server url="ldap://localhost:389/o=example"
   manager-dn="uid=admin,ou=system"
   manager-password="secret" />
```

Add this code in the `beans` tag of the xml. Here we are specifying the authentication mechanism as basic and the user information is stored the LDAP server.

Edit the `web.xml` file:

```
<context-param>
  <param-name>contextConfigLocation</param-name>
  <param-value>
    /WEB-INF/spring-security.xml
  </param-value>
</context-param>

<listener>
  <listener-class>
    org.springframework.web.context.ContextLoaderListener
  </listener-class>
</listener>
```

We have to configure `springsecurityFilterchain` as shown in the previous examples.

How it works...

Now access the following URL:

```
http://127.0.0.1:8888/springgwtldapsecurity.html?gwt.
codesvr=127.0.0.1:9997
```

Enter the login username and password and you will be taken to the GWT page. Spring will use the details provided in `<ldap-server>` tag to gain access to open LDAP. Spring Security LDAP will talk to open LDAP and the user-entered values will be checked with retrieved values for authentication. On success, the user is redirected to the application. With this, we can see that GWT seamlessly integrates with Spring Security.

There's more...

There is an active project on google `code-gwtsecurity` package, which is meant for Spring Security integration with the GWT application. It offers login via GWT pop-up window. On authentication failure, it gives the error message to the user on the GWT window. The file `Spring4GWT jar` works by intercepting the error message in the RPC.

Let's see how Spring integrates with Vaadin in the next chapter.

6
Spring Security with Vaadin

In this chapter we will cover:

- ▶ Spring Security with Vaadin – basic authentication
- ▶ Spring Security with Vaadin – Spring form-based authentication
- ▶ Spring Security with Vaadin – customized JSP form-based authentication
- ▶ Spring Security with Vaadin – using Vaadin form

Introduction

Vaadin has emerged as a popular framework in current projects. It offers RIA just like GWT-rich Internet applications. It doesn't have the RPC calls and those async service classes. It works similar to GWT widgets. Vaadin also integrates easily with portlets. In GWT we had to install browser compatible GWT plugin but in Vaadin we don't need to do that. The application developed in Vaadin is compatible on all modern browsers. Vaadin can be written as server side and client side applications. The Vaadin UI component is actually a JavaServlet component which easily runs on web servers such as Tomcat and also application servers like JBOSS and Glassfish. For the current demonstration I am using Tomcat and Eclipse Indigo.

In this chapter we will demonstrate Spring Security with Vaadin integration using various approaches. Let's first do a basic setup for this. It's all about downloading the plugin and creating a sample Vaadin project.

Spring Security with Vaadin – basic authentication

Our aim is to do a simple basic authentication on the Vaadin application. I want a login dialog to pop up when we access the URL of the Vaadin application. I have created a simple product catalog application which looks very similar to the address book.

Getting ready

- Set up Vaadin application on Eclipse:

    - Download Vaadin `http://vaadin.com/eclipse` for Eclipse Indigo.

    For this chapter we will demonstrate Spring Security integration with both the Vaadin versions (Vaadin 6 and Vaadin 7).

    - Create a Vaadin web project in Eclipse with Vaadin 7—this will generate a default application with a click button which we will modify.

    - Run the application on the Tomcat server.

- Create an `applicationContext.xml` file. It is mandatory to name it as `applicationContext`, or else we will get error messages in the console.

- Edit the `web.xml` file with spring listeners.

- Add all the jars in the class-path.

How to do it...

The following steps are for integrating Spring Security with Vaadin to demonstrate basic authentication:

1. Update the `web.xml` file with spring listener and spring filter, with Vaadin servlet:

```
<display-name>Vaadin_Project1</display-name>
<filter>
  <filter-name>springSecurityFilterChain</filter-name>
  <filter-class>org.springframework.web.filter.
    DelegatingFilterProxy</filter-class>
</filter>

<filter-mapping>
  <filter-name>springSecurityFilterChain</filter-name>
  <url-pattern>/*</url-pattern>
</filter-mapping>
```

```xml
<listener>
  <listener-class>
    org.springframework.web.context.ContextLoaderListener
  </listener-class>
</listener>

<context-param>
  <description>
  Vaadin production mode</description>
  <param-name>productionMode</param-name>
  <param-value>false</param-value>
</context-param>

<servlet>
  <servlet-name>Vaadin_Project1</servlet-name>
  <servlet-class>com.vaadin.server.VaadinServlet
    </servlet-class>
<init-param>
  <description>
    Vaadin UI class to use</description>
  <param-name>UI</param-name>
  <param-value>com.example.vaadin_project1
    .Vaadin_project1UI</param-value>
</init-param>
<init-param>
  <description>
  Legacy mode to return the value of
    the property as a string from
    AbstractProperty.toString()</description>
  <param-name>legacyPropertyToString</param-name>
  <param-value>false</param-value>
</init-param>
</servlet>
<servlet-mapping>
  <servlet-name>Vaadin_Project1</servlet-name>
  <url-pattern>/*</url-pattern>
</servlet-mapping>
```

2. You can observe that we haven't configured `<context-param>` as we did in our previous applications. Spring will automatically look for the `applicationContext.xml` file. For setting up Vaadin we need to configure the Vaadin servlet class with two parameters `PropertyToString` and a UI class named `com.example.vaadin_project1`. Edit the `applicationContext.xml` file using the following code:

```xml
<http auto-config="true">
  <intercept-url pattern="/Vaadin_Project1/**"
    access="ROLE_EDITOR"/>
```

```
<intercept-url pattern="/Vaadin_Project1/*.*"
    access="ROLE_EDITOR"/>
<intercept-url pattern="/**" access="ROLE_EDITOR" />
<http-basic />
</http>

<authentication-manager>
  <authentication-provider>
    <user-service>
      <user name="anjana" password="123456"
          authorities="ROLE_EDITOR" />
    </user-service>
  </authentication-provider>
</authentication-manager>
</beans:beans>
```

This is a simple configuration for basic authentication. With this configuration we expect a login dialog box before showing the Vaadin application. I have created a new role editor.

Here we have created a `ProductList` component to display a list of products.

How it works...

In this example we are demonstrating a basic authentication mechanism with the Vaadin application. Sometimes we do not need to display a jsp page or a Vaadin login form for the user, in such cases we go for basic authentication in which a dialog box pops up requesting the user to enter their credentials. On success, the user is given access to the Vaadin application. Workflow of the application is given as follows:

Now access the following URL:

```
http://localhost:8086/Vaadin_Project1/
```

You should see pages as shown in the following screenshots:

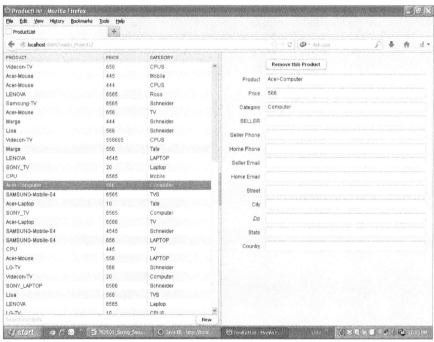

See also

▸ The *Spring Security with Vaadin – Spring form-based authentication* recipe

▸ The *Spring Security with Vaadin – customized JSP form-based authentication* recipe

▸ The *Spring Security with Vaadin – using Vaadin form* recipe

Spring Security with Vaadin – Spring form-based authentication

We will demonstrate form-based authentication in Vaadin. It's very similar to the authentication that we used in our previous recipes. We will be editing the `applicationContext.xml` file. We are not creating any customized login form, we would like to use spring internal login form.

Getting ready

You have to comment the `<http-basic/>` tag from the `application-Context.xml` file.

How to do it...

Edit the `applicationContext.xml` file as shown in the following code:

```
<http auto-config="true">
  <intercept-url pattern="/Vaadin_Project1/**"
    access="ROLE_EDITOR"/>
  <intercept-url pattern="/Vaadin_Project1/*.*"
    access="ROLE_EDITOR"/>
  <intercept-url pattern="/**" access="ROLE_EDITOR" />
</http>
<authentication-manager>
  <authentication-provider>
    <user-service>
      <user name="anjana" password="123456"
      authorities="ROLE_EDITOR" />
    </user-service>
  </authentication-provider>
</authentication-manager>
```

How it works...

In this example spring's internal login form is invoked for authenticating the Vaadin application. This configuration is done in the `applicationConext.xml` file. The Spring framework pops up its own internal jsp file for the user. When the user enters the credentials and clicks on **Submit** they are redirected to the Vaadin application. Run the Tomcat server.

Now access the following URL:

```
http://localhost:8086/Vaadin_Project1/
```

This is a Spring provided inbuilt login form.

Enter the login username and password and you will be taken to the Vaadin product list.

Similarly you can authenticate using the database and LDAP just by editing the authentication-manager configurations.

See also

▶ The *Spring Security with Vaadin – customized JSP form-based authentication* recipe
▶ The *Spring Security with Vaadin – using Vaadin form* recipe

Spring Security with Vaadin – customized JSP form-based authentication

So far we have demonstrated the Vaadin 7 application with the Spring Security API login form and login pop up dialog box. All that we did was create users in the application context file.

This time we will give a different name to the application context and give it a customized login form and use the Vaadin 6 project.

Getting ready

- ▸ Create a sample Vaadin 6 project
- ▸ Add the Spring related jars in the build path
- ▸ Add the Spring Security related jars
- ▸ Add the `vaadin-spring-security.xml` file
- ▸ Add the `mybeans.xml` file
- ▸ Edit the `web.xml` file as shown in the previous section
- ▸ Also add the Spring related jars in the `web-inf lib` folder

How to do it...

The following steps are for implementing a form-based authentication using a customized JSP with the Vaadin application.

Since the entry point is `AbstractApplicationServlet` for the Vaadin 6 application, we will create a class that extends `AbstractApplicationServlet`. This will give us an option to override the methods of the class.

We will also create a class that extends the `Application` class. In this class we will create a window. For example, we will just add some text after login.

We will also add jsp file mapping in the `web.xml` file.

We need to map the `MyAbstractApplicationServlet` class as a Servlet in the file `web.xml`.

We also need to configure the Spring context listeners and Spring filters.

1. Edit the `web.xml` file:

```
<display-name>Vaadin_Project3</display-name>
  <context-param>
    <description>Vaadin production mode</description>
    <param-name>productionMode</param-name>
    <param-value>true</param-value>
  </context-param>
  <context-param>
    <param-name>contextConfigLocation</param-name>
    <param-value>
      /WEB-INF/vaadin-spring-security.xml
      /WEB-INF/mybeans.xml
    </param-value>
```

```xml
  </context-param>

  <servlet>
    <servlet-name>login</servlet-name>
    <jsp-file>/jsp/login.jsp</jsp-file>
  </servlet>

  <servlet>
    <servlet-name>login_error</servlet-name>
    <jsp-file>/jsp/login_error.jsp</jsp-file>
  </servlet>

  <servlet-mapping>
    <servlet-name>login</servlet-name>
    <url-pattern>/jsp/login</url-pattern>
  </servlet-mapping>

  <servlet-mapping>
    <servlet-name>login_error</servlet-name>
    <url-pattern>/jsp/login_error</url-pattern>
  </servlet-mapping>

  <servlet>
    <servlet-name>Vaadin Application Servlet</servlet-name>
    <servlet-class>packt.vaadin.
      MyAbstractApplicationServlet</servlet-class>
  </servlet>

  <servlet-mapping>
    <servlet-name>Vaadin Application Servlet</servlet-name>
    <url-pattern>/*</url-pattern>
  </servlet-mapping>
```

2. Edit the `vaadin-spring-security.xml` file:

```xml
<global-method-security pre-post-annotations="enabled" />

<http auto-config='true'>
  <intercept-url pattern="/jsp/login*"
    access="IS_AUTHENTICATED_ANONYMOUSLY" />
  <intercept-url pattern="/jsp/login_error*"
    access="IS_AUTHENTICATED_ANONYMOUSLY" />
  <intercept-url pattern="/**" access="ROLE_USER" />
  <form-login login-page='/jsp/login'
    authentication-failure-url="/jsp/login_error" />
</http>
```

```
<authentication-manager>
  <authentication-provider>
    <user-service>
      <user name="raghu" password="anju"
         authorities="ROLE_USER,ROLE_ADMIN" />
      <user name="onju" password="bonju"
         authorities="ROLE_USER" />
    </user-service>
  </authentication-provider>
</authentication-manager>
```

3. Subclass and override the method `AbstractApplicationServlet`.

   The `AbstractApplicationServlet` class is an abstract class that extends `HttpServlet` and implements an interface called *Constants*. The `Service()` and `init()` methods are the servlet methods which are used by the servlet container. We have created an `appContext` object and have initialized it in the `init ()` method. The `getNewApplication()` method has been overridden to get the class that extends the application. The `getApplication()` method has been overridden.

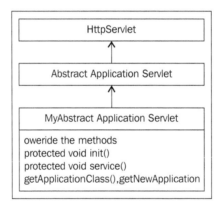

4. The implementation is given as follows:

   `MyAbstractApplicationServlet`

```
public class MyAbstractApplicationServlet extends
  AbstractApplicationServlet
{
  private WebApplicationContext appContext;
  private Class<? extends Application> applicationClass;

  @Override
  protected Application getNewApplication
    (HttpServletRequest httpServletRequest) throws
      ServletException {
```

```
    MainApplication mainApplication = (MainApplication)
      appContext.getBean("applicationBean");
    mainApplication.setWebApplicationContext(appContext);
    return  mainApplication;
  }

  @Override
  protected void service(HttpServletRequest request
    , HttpServletResponse response)
      throws ServletException, IOException {
    super.service(request, response);
  }

  @Override
  public void init(ServletConfig servletConfig)
      throws ServletException {
    super.init(servletConfig);
    appContext = WebApplicationContextUtils
      .getWebApplicationContext
      (servletConfig.getServletContext());
  }

  @Override
  protected Class<? extends Application>
    getApplicationClass() throws ClassNotFoundException {
    return MainApplication.class;
  }
}
}
```

5. Subclass and override the method `ApplicationClass`.

   `ApplicationClass` is an abstract class which implements some interfaces. We have overridden the `init()` method of the abstract class. You have to create the `HeaderHorizontalLayout` classes and add them as components to the window.

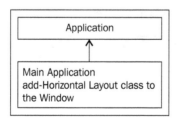

MainApplication

```
@Component("applicationBean")
@Scope("prototype")
```

```
public class MainApplication extends Application {

    public WebApplicationContext webappContext;

    @Override
    public void init() {
      Window window;
      window = new Window("My Vaadin Application");
      window.addComponent(new HeaderHorizontalLayout(this));
      window.addComponent(new BodyHorizontalLayout(this));
      window.addComponent(new FooterHorizontalLayout(this));
      setMainWindow(window);
    }


    public void setWebApplicationContext
      (WebApplicationContext appContext){
    this.webappContext = webappContext;
    }

}
```

How it works...

In this example we are using the customized jsp page to handle the access to the Vaadin application. The customized jsp is displayed to the user when user tries to access the Vaadin application. The user enters the username and password which is then authenticated by the Spring framework. On successful authentication the Vaadin page is displayed.

The workflow is given as follows:

Now access the URL:

```
http://localhost:8086/Vaadin_Project3/
```

Enter the login username and password you will be taken to the Vaadin page.

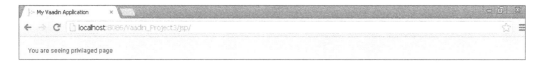

See also

▸ The *Spring Security with Vaadin – using Vaadin form* recipe

Spring Security with Vaadin – using Vaadin form

So far we have used the customized JSP page or the Spring-provided login pop up box or the jsp file. We have also demonstrated Spring Security integration with both Vaadin 6 and Vaadin 7. So I was tempted to provide a complete Vaadin with Spring Security implementation. Let's create a Vaadin form and we will integrate it with Spring Security.

Getting ready

▸ Create a Vaadin 7 project in your Eclipse IDE

▸ Create a `MyLoginView` class that extends the panel

▸ Create a `SecuredView` class that extends the panel

▸ Create a `MyVaadinServlet` class that extends `VaadinServlet`

▸ Create a `VaadinRequestHolder` class

▸ Configure the `web.xml` file

▸ Edit the `applicationContext.xml` file

▸ Implement the `View` interface for the panel classes

How to do it...

The steps given as follows are for creating a Vaadin login form and using it for authenticating the user with Spring Security:

1. `MyLoginView` for the login form will be loaded on application start up.

   ```
   public class MyLoginView extends Panel implements View {
     private Layout mainLayout;
     Navigator navigator;
   ```

```java
protected static final String CountView = "SecuredView";
public MyLoginView() {
  final FormLayout loginlayout=new FormLayout();
  final TextField nameField=new TextField("name");
  final PasswordField passwordField=
    new PasswordField("password");
  loginlayout.addComponent(nameField);
  loginlayout.addComponent(passwordField);
  Button loginButton = new Button("Login");
  loginlayout.addComponent(loginButton);
  mainLayout = new VerticalLayout();
  mainLayout.addComponent(loginlayout);
  setContent(mainLayout);

  loginButton.addClickListener(new Button.ClickListener() {
    public void buttonClick(ClickEvent event) {
      try{
        ServletContext servletContext =
        VaadinRequestHolder.getRequest()
        .getSession().getServletContext();
        UsernamePasswordAuthenticationToken token =
          new UsernamePasswordAuthenticationToken(
          nameField.getValue(),passwordField.getValue());
          token.setDetails( new WebAuthenticationDetails
            (VaadinRequestHolder.getRequest()));
          WebApplicationContext wac =
            WebApplicationContextUtils.getRequired
            WebApplicationContext(servletContext);
          AuthenticationManager authManager =
            wac.getBean(AuthenticationManager.class);
          Authentication authentication =
            authManager.authenticate(token);
          SecurityContextHolder.getContext()
            .setAuthentication(authentication);
          if(authentication.isAuthenticated()){
            Notification.show("You are authenticated");
          navigator = new Navigator(getUI().getCurrent()
            , mainLayout);
          navigator.addView(CountView, new SecuredView());
          navigator.navigateTo(CountView);
        }

      } catch (BadCredentialsException e) {
```

```
        Notification.show("Bad credentials");
      }
    }
  });


  }
  @Override
  public void enter(ViewChangeEvent event) {
  }
```

We have used the form layout and have added the username and password fields. We have added a button. On a button click we are doing authentication.

We are capturing the `VaadinRequest` object in the `requestHolder`. `UserNamePasswords`. The authentication token receives the input from the username and password fields. The token is then passed to the `AuthenticationManger` to authenticate the fields. If authentication is successful it will navigate to the secured page. It will also give notification to the user.

2. `Secured View` is to be used after authentication and to provide logout functionality.

```
public class SecuredView extends Panel implements View {
  public static final String NAME = "count";
  private Layout mainLayout;
  Navigator navigator;
  protected static final String MainView = "LoginView";
  public SecuredView() {
    mainLayout = new VerticalLayout();
    mainLayout.addComponent(new Label
      ("You are seeing a secured page"));
    Button logoutButton = new Button("Logout");
    mainLayout.addComponent(logoutButton);
    setContent(mainLayout);
    logoutButton.addClickListener(new Button.
      ClickListener() {
    public void buttonClick(ClickEvent event) {
    try{
      ServletContext servletContext = VaadinRequestHolder
        .getRequest().getSession().getServletContext();
      WebApplicationContext wac =
        WebApplicationContextUtils
        .getRequiredWebApplicationContext(servletContext);
      LogoutHandler logoutHandler = wac.getBean
        (LogoutHandler.class);
```

```
        Authentication authentication =
          SecurityContextHolder.
          getContext().getAuthentication();
        logoutHandler.logout(VaadinRequestHolder.getRequest()
          , null, authentication);

        Notification.show("You are logged out");
        navigator = new Navigator
          (getUI().getCurrent(), mainLayout);
        navigator.addView(MainView, new MyLoginView());
        navigator.navigateTo(MainView);
      } catch (BadCredentialsException e) {

        Notification.show("Bad credentials");
        }
      }
    });
    }

public void enter(ViewChangeEvent event) {


}

}
```

The secured view has a label and a logout button. The logout button click event handles the `springlogout`. On logout the user is re-directed to the login page. The `LogoutHandler` class has a `logout ()` method that handles the authentication. I have used the navigator class. You can create an instance of navigator with UI class `getUI.Current` that gives a UI object.

This approach can be used in your panel classes. I have also passed the layout object to the constructor.

```
navigator = new Navigator(getUI().getCurrent(),
    mainLayout);
navigator.addView(MainView, new MyLoginView());
navigator.navigateTo(MainView);
```

A pictorial representation of the two classes is given as follows:

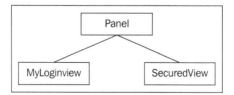

3. Extend the Vaadin servlet to capture the request object.

```
MyVaadinServlet
public class MyVaadinServlet extends VaadinServlet {
  @Override
  protected void service(HttpServletRequest request,
    HttpServletResponse response) throws ServletException,
    IOException {
  SecurityContextHolder.setContext
    (SecurityContextHolder.createEmptyContext());
  VaadinRequestHolder.setRequest(request);
  super.service(request, response);
  VaadinRequestHolder.clean();
  SecurityContextHolder.clearContext();
  }
}
```

The Vaadin servlet is configured in the `web.xml` file. It accepts the UI class as a parameter. In the previous code we have extended the Vaadin servlet and have overridden the `service ()` method, in which we are passing the request to the `VaadinRequestHolder` class. By doing this we will be passing the context object to `SecurityContextHolder` to start with the authentication.

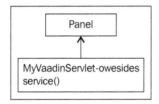

4. Register the views in the UI class.

```
Vaadin_project5UI
@SuppressWarnings("serial")
@Theme("vaadin_project5")
public class Vaadin_project5UI extends UI{
  private Layout mainLayout;
  Navigator navigator;
  protected static final String CountView = "main";
  @Override
  protected void init(VaadinRequest request) {
    getPage().setTitle("Navigation Example");
    // Create a navigator to control the views
    navigator = new Navigator(this, this);
    // Create and register the views
    navigator.addView("", new MyLoginView());
```

```
        navigator.addView(CountView, new SecuredView());
    }
}
```

In this code we are registering the `LoginView` and the `SecuredView` and the default login view will be called.

5. Configuring the `web.xml` file:

```xml
<display-name>Vaadin_Project5</display-name>
<context-param>
  <description>
  Vaadin production mode</description>
  <param-name>productionMode</param-name>
  <param-value>false</param-value>
</context-param>
<servlet>
  <servlet-name>Vaadin_project5 Application</servlet-name>
  <servlet-class>com.example.vaadin_project5.MyVaadinServlet
    </servlet-class>
  <init-param>
    <description>
    Vaadin UI class to use</description>
    <param-name>UI</param-name>
    <param-value>com.example.vaadin_project5.
      Vaadin_project5UI</param-value>
  </init-param>
  <init-param>
    <description>
    Legacy mode to return the value of the property
      as a string from AbstractProperty.toString()
      </description>
    <param-name>legacyPropertyToString</param-name>
    <param-value>false</param-value>
  </init-param>
</servlet>
<servlet-mapping>
  <servlet-name>Vaadin_project5 Application</servlet-name>
  <url-pattern>/*</url-pattern>
</servlet-mapping>
<listener>
  <listener-class>org.springframework.
    web.context.ContextLoaderListener</listener-class>
</listener>
</web-app>
```

We have configured `MyVaadinServlet` in `web.xml`.

6. Edit the `application-Context.xml` file.

```
<global-method-security pre-post-annotations="enabled" />
<authentication-manager>
  <authentication-provider>
    <user-service>
    <user name="anjana" password="123456"
       authorities="ROLE_EDITOR" />
    </user-service>
  </authentication-provider>
</authentication-manager>
<beans:bean class="org.springframework.security
  .web.authentication.logout.
  SecurityContextLogoutHandler">
  <beans:property name="invalidateHttpSession"
     value="false" />
</beans:bean>
</beans:beans>
```

How it works...

In this example we have created a Vaadin login form. This is another option for creating a login form using the Vaadin framework classes if the developer doesn't want to use external jsp. This will make it a pure Vaadin application with a Spring Security application. The user is authenticated and authorized by Spring Security before showing the actual product catalog page. The Vaadin form submits the users' credentials to the Spring Security framework which does the authentication and authorization. The `MyVaadinServlet` class communicates with the Spring Security context to set the security context with the Vaadin application.

The workflow of Spring Security with Vaadin is given as follows:

▶ Run the Tomcat server.

▶ Now access the URL:

```
http://localhost:8086/Vaadin_Project5/
```

The following screenshot shows the Vaadin login form:

It also displays a message for bad credentials:

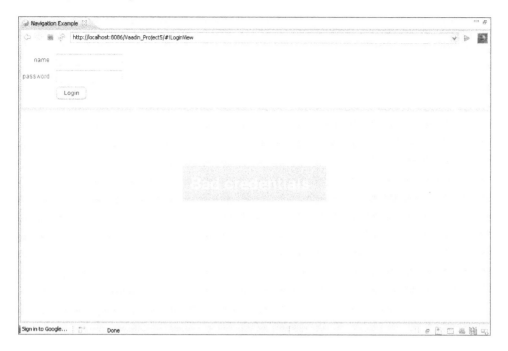

After authentication you will be navigated to the secured page:

Clicking on **Logout** you will be taken back to login view. The following screenshot displays the information:

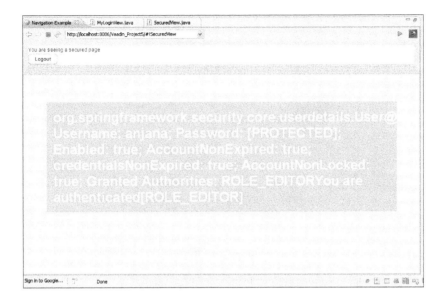

7
Spring Security with Wicket

In this chapter we will cover:

- ▶ Spring Security with Wicket – basic database authentication
- ▶ Spring Security with Wicket – Spring form-based database authentication
- ▶ Spring Security with Wicket – customized JSP form-based database authentication
- ▶ Spring authentication with Wicket authorization
- ▶ Multitenancy using Wicket and Spring Security

Introduction

Before starting up Wicket, we were checking the available versions. The latest one is 6.9. It is clearly mentioned in the Apache Wicket site that the latest projects should use Version 6.9 as the base. We have NetBeans 7.1 after downloading the Wicket plugin for net beans. We found that the net beans Wicket plugin supports Version 1.5 of Wicket.

We prefer using the latest stable version; it will have many bug fixes and upgrades and will make it easier to develop.

Wicket also uses the *Wicket filter* to dispatch requests and responses. Just as with GWT and Vaadin applications, which had servlet, which expected some parameters such as UI class to get initialized, we need to provide a class name of the class that extends the `Web Application` class as a parameter to the filter. Then there are classes, which extend the `WebPage` class. It's a good convention and practice to create an HTML page with the same name as the class that extends the `WebPage` class.

Wicket uses the multilevel inheritance approach. We have to extend the `Wicket` class to achieve various scenarios. It also has a built-in authentication and authorization API.

Setting up a database

The following code will set up a database:

```
CREATE TABLE `users1` (
  `USER_ID` INT(10) UNSIGNED NOT NULL,
  `USERNAME` VARCHAR(45) NOT NULL,
  `PASSWORD` VARCHAR(45) NOT NULL,
  `ENABLED` tinyint(1) NOT NULL,
  PRIMARY KEY (`USER_ID`)
) ENGINE=InnoDB DEFAULT CHARSET=utf8;
CREATE TABLE `user_roles` (
  `USER_ROLE_ID` INT(10) UNSIGNED NOT NULL,
  `USER_ID` INT(10) UNSIGNED NOT NULL,
  `AUTHORITY` VARCHAR(45) NOT NULL,
  PRIMARY KEY (`USER_ROLE_ID`),
  KEY `FK_user_roles` (`USER_ID`),
  CONSTRAINT `FK_user_roles` FOREIGN KEY (`USER_ID`)
    REFERENCES `users` (`USER_ID`)
) ENGINE=InnoDB DEFAULT CHARSET=utf8;
```

Setting up the Wicket application

The following statement is the Maven command that needs to be executed. You should have Maven installed on your machine and should have a local repository. By default, it is in `.m2\repository`. After running the command, you should get build success that gives us a green signal to start with Wicket implementation:

```
mvn archetype:generate -DarchetypeGroupId=org.apache.
wicket -DarchetypeArtifactId=wicket-archetype-quickstart
-DarchetypeVersion=6.9.1 -DgroupId=com.packt -DartifactId=spring-
security-wicket -DarchetypeRepository=https://repository.apache.org/
-DinteractiveMode=false
```

The following output is visible on the command prompt:

```
[INFO] Parameter: groupId, Value: com.packt

[INFO] Parameter: artifactId, Value: spring-security-wicket

[INFO] Parameter: version, Value: 1.0-SNAPSHOT

[INFO] Parameter: package, Value: com.packt

[INFO] Parameter: packageInPathFormat, Value: com/packt

[INFO] Parameter: version, Value: 1.0-SNAPSHOT

[INFO] Parameter: package, Value: com.packt
```

```
[INFO] Parameter: groupId, Value: com.packt
[INFO] Parameter: artifactId, Value: spring-security-wicket
[INFO] project created from Archetype in dir: E:\spring-security-wicket
[INFO] ------------------------------------------------------------------------
[INFO] BUILD SUCCESS
[INFO] ------------------------------------------------------------------------
[INFO] Total time: 1:22.610s
[INFO] Finished at: Mon Jul 15 21:17:24 IST 2013
[INFO] Final Memory: 7M/13M
[INFO] ------------------------------------------------------------------------
```

The following commands will finish the complete set up of Wicket. They will also download the Wicket framework source files into the repository.

```
Spring-security-wicket>mvn clean compile install
Spring-security-wicket>mvn tomcat:run
Spring-security-wicket>mvn eclipse: eclipse
```

Access the following URL:

```
http://localhost:8080/spring-security-wicket/
```

The URL will display the welcome page of the Wicket application. Wicket application setup is ready.

Wicket also comes with its own authentication and authorization API. Let's see how we can use it.

Spring Security with Wicket – basic database authentication

Our aim is to do a simple basic authentication on the Wicket application. I want a login dialog to pop-up when we access the URL of the Wicket application. On success it should get redirected to the home page. We need to add Spring Security dependencies to the pom.xml file and rebuild the Wicket application. The next step will be configuring the spring listener in the web.xml file. We also need to add the applicationContext.xml file.

Getting ready

- Update the `pom.xml` file with Spring dependency.
- Create an `applicationContext.xml` file. It's mandatory to name it as `applicationContext` or else we will get error messages in the console.
- Edit the `web.xml` with Spring listeners.
- Create a `database-details.xml` file and add the database details.
- Add the `db-details.xml` file as `context-param` to the spring listener.

How to do it...

The following are the steps for implementing Spring Security with Wicket to demonstrate basic authentication where credentials are stored in the database:

1. Add dependency to the `POM.xml` file:

```xml
<!-- Spring dependecncies -->
<dependency>
    <groupId>org.springframework</groupId>
    <artifactId>spring-core</artifactId>
    <version>${spring.version}</version>
</dependency>

<dependency>
    <groupId>org.springframework</groupId>
    <artifactId>spring-web</artifactId>
    <version>${spring.version}</version>
</dependency>

<dependency>
    <groupId>org.springframework</groupId>
    <artifactId>spring-webmvc</artifactId>
    <version>${spring.version}</version>
</dependency>

<!-- Spring Security -->
<dependency>
    <groupId>org.springframework.security</groupId>
    <artifactId>spring-security-core</artifactId>
    <version>${spring.version}</version>
</dependency>
```

```xml
<dependency>
  <groupId>org.springframework.security</groupId>
  <artifactId>spring-security-web</artifactId>
  <version>${spring.version}</version>
</dependency>

<dependency>
  <groupId>org.springframework.security</groupId>
  <artifactId>spring-security-config</artifactId>
  <version>${spring.version}</version>
</dependency>
<!-- WICKET DEPENDENCIES -->
<dependency>
  <groupId>org.apache.wicket</groupId>
  <artifactId>wicket-core</artifactId>
  <version>${wicket.version}</version>
</dependency>
<!-- WICKET Authentication-DEPENDENCIES -->
<dependency>
  <groupId>org.apache.wicket</groupId>
  <artifactId>wicket-auth-roles</artifactId>
  <version>6.9.1</version>
</dependency>
```

2. Update the `Web.xml` file with Spring listener and the Spring filter with Wicket filter:

```xml
<filter>
  <filter-name>springSecurityFilterChain</filter-name>
  <filter-class>
    org.springframework.web.filter.DelegatingFilterProxy
    </filter-class>
</filter>

<filter-mapping>
  <filter-name>springSecurityFilterChain</filter-name>
  <url-pattern>/*</url-pattern>
</filter-mapping>

<listener>
  <listener-class>
    org.springframework.web.context.ContextLoaderListener
    </listener-class>
</listener>
```

```xml
<filter>
  <filter-name>wicket.spring-security-wicket</filter-name>
<filter-class>
  org.apache.wicket.protocol.http.WicketFilter
    </filter-class>
  <init-param>
    <param-name>applicationClassName</param-name>
    <param-value>com.packt.WicketApplication</param-value>
  </init-param>
</filter>

<filter-mapping>
  <filter-name>wicket.spring-security-wicket</filter-name>
  <url-pattern>/*</url-pattern>
</filter-mapping>
```

3. Edit the `applicationContext.xml` file:

```xml
<global-method-security pre-post-annotations="enabled" />

<http auto-config="true">
  <intercept-url pattern="/spring-security-wicket/**"
    access="ROLE_SELLER"/>
  <intercept-url pattern="/spring-security-wicket/*.*"
    access="ROLE_SELLER"/>
  <intercept-url pattern="/**"access="ROLE_SELLER" />
  <http-basic />
</http>

<authentication-manager>
  <authentication-provider>
    <jdbc-user-service data-source-ref="MySqlDS"
      users-by-username-query="
      select username,password, enabled
      from users1 where username=?"
      authorities-by-username-query="
      select u.username, ur.role from users1 u,
        user_roles ur
    where u.user_id = ur.user_id and u.username =?  " />
  </authentication-provider>
</authentication-manager>
```

This is a simple configuration for basic authentication. With this configuration we expect a login dialog box before showing the Wicket application. I have created a new role, seller.

How it works...

Now access the following URL:

```
http://localhost:8080/spring-security-wicket/
```

This is the initial setup example of integrating Spring Security with Wicket. We have demonstrated the basic authentication mechanism. Access to the Wicket application is interrupted with Spring Security by the Login form. On successful authentication, the user gains access to the wicket application.

The page displayed is shown in the following screenshot:

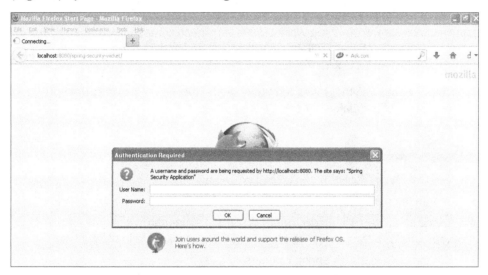

- ▶ The *Spring Security with Wicket – spring form-based authentication* recipe
- ▶ The *Spring Security with Wicket – customized JSP form-based authentication* recipe
- ▶ The *Spring authentication with Wicket authorization* recipe
- ▶ The *Multitenancy using Wicket and Spring Security* recipe

Spring Security with Wicket – Spring form-based database authentication

In our previous recipe we found the Wicket 6.9 is very much compatible with Spring Security and it was very easy to integrate. All we did was to add spring dependency and we configured the `applicationContext.xml` file.

In this section we shall use the Spring form to do authentication. We expect the Spring form to show up in place of the dialog box and do the authentication for us.

Getting ready

- ▶ Create a Maven Wicket project: `spring-security-wicket_springform`.
- ▶ Update the `pom.xml` file with Spring dependency.
- ▶ Create an `applicationContext.xml` file. It's mandatory to name it as `applicationContext` or else we will get error messages in the console.
- ▶ Edit the `web.xml` with Spring listeners.
- ▶ Create a database `details.xml` file and add the database details.
- ▶ Add the file as a context parameter to the Spring listener.

How to do it...

Edit the `applicationContext.xml` file using the following code:

```
<global-method-security pre-post-annotations="enabled" />

<http auto-config="true">
  <intercept-url pattern="/spring-security-wicket/**"
    access="ROLE_SELLER"/>
  <intercept-url pattern="/spring-security-wicket/*.*"
    access="ROLE_SELLER"/>
```

```
      <intercept-url pattern="/**" access="ROLE_SELLER" />
   </http>

   <authentication-manager>
     <authentication-provider>
       <jdbc-user-service data-source-ref="MySqlDS"
       users-by-username-query="
       select username,password, enabled
       from users1 where username=?"

       authorities-by-username-query="
       select u.username, ur.role from users1 u, user_roles ur
       where u.user_id = ur.user_id and u.username =?  " />
     </authentication-provider>
   </authentication-manager>
```

This is a simple configuration for form authentication. With this configuration we expect a **Login Page** before showing the Wicket application. The only change is that we have removed the `<http-basic>` tag for the previous application. Also observe the URL, which will have a session ID.

How it works...

Now access the following URL:

`http://localhost:8080/spring-security-wicket_springform/`

In this example we are showing how to invoke Spring's internal login form in a Wicket application. When we access the Wicket application, we will be redirected to Spring's own login page. The user enters their username and password which will be authenticated and authorized by the Spring's authentication provider. On success, the user gains access to the Wicket application.

You should see the following screen when you access the above URL:

See also

▸ The *Spring Security with Wicket – customized JSP form-based authentication* recipe

▸ The *Spring authentication with Wicket authorization* recipe

▸ The *Multitenancy using Wicket and Spring Security* recipe

Spring Security with Wicket – customized JSP form-based database authentication

The previous two recipes were to test the compatibility of Wicket with Spring Security. It also demonstrates how easy it is to integrate spring with Wicket. We learned from our two Wicket recipes that we can easily use Spring-basic and Spring-form-based authentication with a database and the same can be extended to LDAP as well.

In this recipe we are going to add a customized JSP form. We expect the Wicket application to call our JSP form for login. If the developer doesn't want to create a Wicket form, they can use this approach. This approach also holds good for GWT and Vaadin.

You also need to give anonymous access to the login page.

Getting ready

▸ Create a Maven Wicket project: `spring-security-wicket_customized_jsp`.

▸ Update the `pom.xml` file with Spring dependency.

▸ Create an `applicationContext.xml` file. It's mandatory to name it as `applicationContext` or else we will get error messages in the console.

▸ Edit the `web.xml` with Spring listeners.

▸ Also add the `login.jsp` configuration as a servlet to `web.xml`.

▸ Create a database, `details.xml` file, and add the database details.

▸ Add the file as a context parameter to the Spring listener.

▸ Also, you need to add a `login.jsp`; you can use the `login.jsp` file used in the previous chapter.

How to do it...

The following steps are for integrating Spring Security with the Wicket framework to demonstrate form-based authentication with a customized JSP:

1. Edit the `applicationContext.xml` file:

```xml
<global-method-security pre-post-annotations="enabled" />

<http auto-config='true'>
  <intercept-url pattern="/jsp/login*"
    access="IS_AUTHENTICATED_ANONYMOUSLY" />
  <intercept-url pattern="/jsp/login_error*"
    access="IS_AUTHENTICATED_ANONYMOUSLY" />
  <intercept-url pattern="/**" access="ROLE_SELLER" />
  <form-login login-page='/jsp/login'
    authentication-failure-url="/jsp/login_error" />
</http>
<authentication-manager>
  <authentication-provider>
    <jdbc-user-service data-source-ref="MySqlDS"
    users-by-username-query="
    select username,password, enabled
    from users1 where username=?"

    authorities-by-username-query="
    select u.username, ur.role from users1 u, user_roles ur
    where u.user_id = ur.user_id and u.username =?  " />
  </authentication-provider>
</authentication-manager>
```

   The customized `login.jsp` has been configured as an anonymous user in the `applicationContext.xml` file.

2. Edit the `web.xml` file:

```xml
<servlet>
  <servlet-name>login</servlet-name>
  <jsp-file>/jsp/login.jsp</jsp-file>
</servlet>

<servlet>
  <servlet-name>login_error</servlet-name>
  <jsp-file>/jsp/login_error.jsp</jsp-file>
</servlet>
```

```
<servlet-mapping>
  <servlet-name>login</servlet-name>
  <url-pattern>/jsp/login</url-pattern>
</servlet-mapping>

<servlet-mapping>
  <servlet-name>login_error</servlet-name>
  <url-pattern>/jsp/login_error</url-pattern>
</servlet-mapping>
```

The `login.jsp` has been configured as a servlet.

How it works...

Now access the following URL:

`http://localhost:8080/spring-security-wicket_springform/`

In this example we are integrating the Wicket application with our own `login.jsp` file to do the authentication and authorization. When the user tries to access the Wicket application, Spring Security interrupts the user from accessing the application that provides the jsp page created and configured in the `applicationContext.xml`. On submit, the Spring Security authentication action is triggered, which does the authentication and authorization. On success, the user gains access to the Wicket application.

You should see the following screenshot when you access this URL:

See also

▸ The *Spring authentication with Wicket authorization* recipe
▸ The *Multitenancy using Wicket and Spring Security* recipe

Spring authentication with Wicket authorization

So far we have seen various options to use Spring Security outside the Wicket application. We shall now see how we can create a security form in the wicket framework and use it with the Spring framework with two different roles. The recipe also demonstrates how we can use Spring beans in the Wicket application.

Getting ready

- Create a Maven Wicket project: `spring-security-wicket`.
- Update the `pom.xml` file with Spring dependency.
- Create an `applicationContext.xml` file. It's mandatory to name it as `applicationContext` or else we will get error messages in the console.
- Add a `spring-wicket-security` dependency.
- Edit the `web.xml` with Spring listeners.
- Create `EditorPage.html` and `AuthorPage.html` and corresponding `EditorPage.java` and `AuthorPage.java` respectively. The author page and the editor page are similar pages but invoked based on roles.
- Create a `HomePage.java` and `HomePage.html`.
- Create `SignInPage.html` and `SignInPage.java`.
- Subclass the `AuthenticatedWebSession` class and override the methods in the super class. By default it uses Wicket authentication, so override it to use Spring authentication.

How to do it...

1. The following step is for implementing authentication with Spring security and authorization with spring Wicket editing the `application-Context.xml`.

   ```
   <!-- Enable annotation scanning -->
   <context:component-scan base-package="com.packt.wicket" />

   </beans>
   ```

2. Edit the `spring-wicket-security.xml` file:

   ```
   <security:authentication-manager alias=
     "springauthenticationManager">
     <security:authentication-provider>
   <!-- TODO change this to reference a real production environment
   user service -->
   ```

```
  <security:user-service>
    <security:user name="jimmy" password=
      "jimmy" authorities="ROLE_EDITOR, ROLE_AUTHOR"/>
    <security:user name="tommy" password=
      "tommy" authorities="ROLE_EDITOR"/>
  </security:user-service>
</security:authentication-provider>
</security:authentication-manager>

<security:global-method-security secured-annotations=
  "enabled" />
```

3. Edit the `AuthorPage.java` file:

```java
@AuthorizeInstantiation("ROLE_AUTHOR")
public class AuthorPage extends WebPage {

  @SpringBean
  private SomeInterfaceImpl someInterfaceImpl;

  public AuthorPage(final PageParameters parameters) {
    super(parameters);
    add(new Label("msg", someInterfaceImpl.method1()));
    add(new Link("Editor"){
      @Override
      public void onClick() {
        Page next = new EditorPage();
        setResponsePage(next);
      }
    });
    add(new Link("Logout"){
      @Override
      public void onClick() {
        getSession().invalidate();
        Page next = new HomePage(parameters);
        setResponsePage(next);
      }
    });
  }
}
```

4. Edit the `SigInPage.java` file:

```java
public final class SignInPage extends WebPage
{
  /**
   * Constructor
```

```
  */
  public SignInPage()
  {
    final SignInForm form = new SignInForm("signinForm");
    add(form);
  }

  /**
   * Sign in form
   */
  public final class SignInForm extends Form<Void>
  {
    private String username;
    private String password;

    public SignInForm(final String id)
    {
      super(id);
      setModel(new CompoundPropertyModel(this));
      add(new RequiredTextField("username"));
      add(new PasswordTextField("password"));
      add(new FeedbackPanel("feedback"));
    }

    @Override
    public final void onSubmit()
    {
      MyWebSession session = getMySession();
      if (session.signIn(username,password))
      {

        setResponsePage(getApplication().getHomePage());

      }
      else
      {
        String errmsg = getString("loginError", null,
          "Unable to sign you in");

      }
    }
    private MyWebSession getMySession()
    {
      return (MyWebSession)getSession();
    }
  }
}
```

5. Edit the `HomePage.java` file:

```java
public class HomePage extends WebPage {
  private static final long serialVersionUID = 1L;
  @SpringBean
  private SomeInterfaceImpl someInterfaceImpl;
  public HomePage(final PageParameters parameters) {
    super(parameters);
    add(new Label("version", getApplication()
      .getFrameworkSettings().getVersion())));
    add(new Label("msg", someInterfaceImpl.method1()));
    add(new Link("click if you are Editor"){
      @Override
      public void onClick() {
        Page next = new EditorPage();
        setResponsePage(next);
      }
    });

    add(new Link("Click if You are Author"){
      @Override
      public void onClick() {
        Page next = new AuthorPage(parameters);
        setResponsePage(next);
      }
    });

  }

}
```

6. Editing the `MyWebSession.java` file:

```java
public class HomePage extends WebPage {
  private static final long serialVersionUID = 1L;
  @SpringBean
  private SomeInterfaceImpl someInterfaceImpl;
  public HomePage(final PageParameters parameters) {
    super(parameters);
    add(new Label("version", getApplication()
      .getFrameworkSettings().getVersion())));
    add(new Label("msg", someInterfaceImpl.method1()));
    add(new Link("click if you are Editor"){
      @Override
      public void onClick() {
        Page next = new EditorPage();
```

```
            setResponsePage(next);
        }
    });

    add(new Link("Click if You are Author"){
      @Override
      public void onClick() {
        Page next = new AuthorPage(parameters);
        setResponsePage(next);
      }
    });


  }


}
```

How it works...

The implementation is very simple; all that we need to do is to have a Wicket sign-in form. After clicking on **submit** we need to get an authenticated session, and this approach will give us an option to integrate Spring security with the Wicket application where we have created a login form using the Wicket application. Spring authenticates the user credentials on success and communicates with the Wicket framework to show the respective authorized pages.

The work flow of the Wicket application with Spring security integration is explained as follows.

When the user clicks on the URL: `http://localhost:8080/spring-security-wicket/`, the user is allowed to access the home page. The home page shows two links, which indicates two different roles and users. After successful authentication the user will be authorized to use respective pages based on the roles. These pages are shown in the following screenshot:

The home page on application startup

Signin Page

Author page

See also

> ▸ The *Multitenancy using Wicket and Spring Security* recipe

Multitenancy using Wicket and Spring Security

Multitenancy has become a popular word with cloud. In a multitenancy setup, each tenant will have a separate datasource. We need to create two different data sources and look ups for the datasource. Let's use a simple Wicket application with a customized JSP, which will have a tenant drop down menu. The user selects a tenant from the drop down menu and a datasource corresponding to the tenant will be set.

I am using NetBeans IDE, which will recognize the Maven projects easily. NetBeans also comes with a glassfish application server and derby database.

Getting ready

- ▸ Update the `login.jsp` file
- ▸ Update the `pom.xml` file with derby database dependency
- ▸ Edit the `applicationContext.xml`
- ▸ Edit the `spring-security.xml`
- ▸ Edit the `web.xml` file
- ▸ Create a filter to capture the tenant ID
- ▸ Also create two databases in derby
- ▸ Create two tables `USERS` and `USER_ROLES` in both databases
- ▸ Add columns in `USERS` (`USER_ID`, `USERNAME`, and `PASSWORD`)
- ▸ Add columns in `USER_ROLES` (`USER_ID`, `USER_ROLE_ID`, and `AUTHORITY`)

How to do it...

The following steps are for implementing multitenancy in a Wicket application with Spring Security API:

1. Edit the `application-Context.xml` file with two data sources:

```xml
<!-- Enable annotation scanning -->
<context:component-scan base-package="com.packt.wicket" />

   <bean id="derbydataSource" class=
     "com.packt.wicket.TenantRoutingDataSource ">
     <property name="targetDataSources">
       <map>
         <entry key="Tenant1" value-ref="tenant1DataSource"/>
         <entry key="Tenant2" value-ref="tenant2DataSource"/>
       </map>
     </property>
   </bean>
   <bean id="tenant1DataSource" class="org.springframework.
     jdbc.datasource.DriverManagerDataSource">
   <property name="driverClassName" value=
     "org.apache.derby.jdbc.EmbeddedDriver" />
   <property name="url" value=
     "jdbc:derby://localhost:1527/client1" />
   <property name="username" value="client1" />
   <property name="password" value="client1" />
```

```
      </bean>
    <bean id="tenant2DataSource" class=
      "org.springframework.jdbc.datasource.
      DriverManagerDataSource">
      <property name="driverClassName" value=
        "org.apache.derby.jdbc.EmbeddedDriver" />
      <property name="url" value=
        "jdbc:derby://localhost:1527/client2" />
      <property name="username" value="client2" />
      <property name="password" value="client2" />

    </bean>
```

2. Edit the `spring-wicket-security.xml` file and also add `ExceptionMappingAuthenticationFailureHandler` bean to capture SQL exceptions:

```
<bean id="authenticationFailureHandler"
  class="org.springframework.security.web.authentication.
  ExceptionMappingAuthenticationFailureHandler">
  <property name="exceptionMappings">
    <props>
      <prop key="org.springframework.security.
        authentication.BadCredentialsException">
        /jsp/login?error='badCredentials'</prop>
      <prop key="org.springframework.security.
        authentication.CredentialsExpiredException">
        /jsp/login?error='credentialsExpired'</prop>
      <prop key="org.springframework.security.
        authentication.LockedException">
        /jsp/login?error='accountLocked'</prop>
      <prop key="org.springframework.security.
        authentication.DisabledException">
        /jsp/login?error='accountDisabled'</prop>
    </props>
  </property>
</bean>
<security:http auto-config='true'>
  <security:intercept-url pattern="/jsp/login*"
    access="IS_AUTHENTICATED_ANONYMOUSLY" />
  <security:intercept-url pattern="/jsp/login_error*"
     access="IS_AUTHENTICATED_ANONYMOUSLY" />
  <security:intercept-url pattern="/**"
    access="ROLE_SELLER" />
  <security:form-login login-page='/jsp/login'
    authentication-failure-handler-
    ref="authenticationFailureHandler" />
```

```
    </security:http>
    <security:authentication-manager>
      <security:authentication-provider>
        <security:jdbc-user-service
          data-source-ref="derbydataSource"
            users-by-username-query=" select
            username,password,'true'
            as enabled from users where username=?"

            authorities-by-username-query="
            select u.username as username, ur.authority as
            authority from users u, user_roles ur
            where u.user_id = ur.user_id and u.username =?"
        />
      </security:authentication-provider>
    </security:authentication-manager>

  <security:global-method-security secured-
    annotations="enabled" />
```

3. Edit the `login.jsp` file:

```
Login here--customized---login page
<form action="/ /Multitenant-spring-security-
  wicket//j_spring_security_check" method="post">
  <table>
    <tr>
      <td>
        User
      </td>
      <td>
        <input name="j_username">
      </td>
    </tr>
    <tr>
      <td>
        Password
      </td>
      <td>
        <input type="password" name="j_password"/>
      </td>
    </tr>

    <tr><td><label>Tenant: </label></td><td>
      <select style="width:146px" id="tenant"
        name="tenant">
```

```
        <option value="">Choose Tenant</option>
        <option value="Tenant1">Tenant 1</option>
        <option value="Tenant2">Tenant
          2</option></select></td>
    </tr>
    <tr>
      <td>
        <input type="submit" value="login">
      </td>
    </tr>
  </table>
</form>
</div>
```

4. Edit the `TenantRoutingDataSource.java` file to route the tenant to a different datasource. The class is a subclass of spring's `AbstractRoutingDataSource`. It is used to set the datasource.

   The URL: `http://docs.spring.io/spring/docs/3.1.x/javadoc-api/org/springframework/jdbc/datasource/lookup/AbstractRoutingDataSource.html`.

```
public class TenantRoutingDataSource extends
  AbstractRoutingDataSource {
  protected final Log logger = LogFactory.getLog
    (this.getClass());

  protected Object determineCurrentLookupKey() {

    String lookupKey = (String)
       ThreadLocalContextUtil.getTenantId();
    System.out.println(lookupKey+"------lookupKey");

    return lookupKey;
  }
}
```

5. Edit `MultitenantFilter` to capture the tenant type and to set the datasource:

```
public void doFilter(ServletRequest request,
   ServletResponse response,FilterChain chain)
   throws IOException, ServletException {
  if (null == filterConfig) {
    return;
  }
  HttpServletRequest httpRequest = (HttpServletRequest)
     request;
```

```
        ThreadLocalContextUtil.clearTenant();
        if (httpRequest.getRequestURI()
          .endsWith(SPRING_SECURITY_LOGOUT_MAPPING)) {
          httpRequest.getSession()
            .removeAttribute(TENANT_HTTP_KEY);
        }

        String tenantID = null;
        if (httpRequest.getRequestURI()
          .endsWith(SPRING_SECURITY_CHECK_MAPPING)) {
          tenantID = request.getParameter(TENANT_HTTP_KEY);
          httpRequest.getSession().setAttribute
            (TENANT_HTTP_KEY, tenantID);
        } else {
          tenantID = (String) httpRequest.getSession()
            .getAttribute(TENANT_HTTP_KEY);
        }

        if (null != tenantID) {
          ThreadLocalContextUtil.setTenantId(tenantID);
          if (logger.isInfoEnabled()) logger.info
            ("Tenant context set with Tenant ID: " + tenantID);
          }

        chain.doFilter(request, response);
    }
```

How it works...

When the user tries to access the application, they will be redirected to the login form in which the user enters their user name and password and selects the tenant. This can also be a company name or location based on business needs. Based on the tenant selected, Spring sets the authentication provider. The `MultitenantFilter` with `TenantRoutingDataSource` class sets the tenant information in the `threadLocalUtil`. The user is authenticated with the tenant data source and is taken to the home page.

Login page on application start up will look as shown in the following screenshots:

Login.page

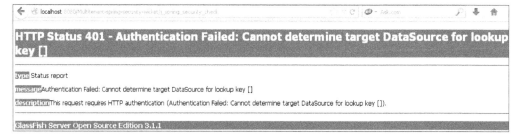

Exception if tenant not

Selected bad credential exception displayed

8

Spring Security with ORM and NoSQL DB

In this chapter we will cover:

- ▸ Spring Security with Hibernate using @preAuthorize annotation
- ▸ Spring Security with Hibernate using authentication provider with @preAuthorize annotation
- ▸ Spring Security with Hibernate using user details service with Derby database
- ▸ Spring Security with MongoDB

Introduction

Spring framework has been designed to easily integrate with ORM frameworks similar to Mybatis, Hibernate, and so on. Hibernate tutorials are very well documented and are available on the JBoss website. Hibernate gives us data persistence.

In this chapter we will see how we can integrate Spring Security with ORM frameworks. We will also integrate Spring Security with the latest MongoDB.

We will first do some basic setup with Hibernate and Spring. Since this chapter has database related stuff we need to create a database for all the recipes used in the chapter. I am using NetBeans IDE with maven. I feel NetBeans IDE is very advanced compared to others.

Setting up the Spring Hibernate application

We will create a simple horror movie application, which will display a list of horror movies with some **CRUD** (**create, read, update, and delete**) functions in the UI. The following steps are involved in setting up a *Spring Hibernate* application:

1. Create a `horrormoviedb` database in Derby. You can use NetBeans.
2. Click on the **Services** tab and you will see **Databases**.
3. Right click to **JavaDB** to see the **Create Database...** option. Select the **Create Database...** option.

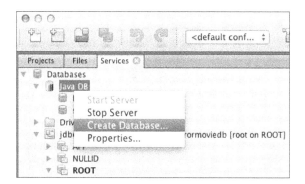

4. Create a table in the database `horrormovie`.

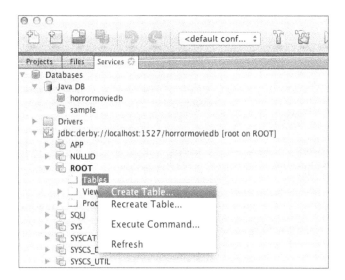

5. Create columns in the table and name the columns as `horrormovie_id`, `horrormovie_name`, and `horrormovie_director`.

6. Create a maven project, update the POM with Spring, Hibernate, Derby and Spring Security dependency, and open it in NetBeans IDE.

7. Create an entity class using `@table` and `@column` annotations.

8. Create a `DAO` and `DAOImpl` class to Handle hibernate operations.

9. Create a `Service` and `ServiceImpl` class to behave like a middle manager between the `DAO` and the UI.

10. Create a controller to handle the UI part.

Spring Security with Hibernate using @preAuthorize annotation

In the current demonstration we are using two different databases. The authentication manager is configured with `tenant1DataSource` which connects to a Derby database which holds the user and role information. Using this data source we will do that authentication and authorization.

For displaying the `horrormovie` list we have created another datasource in Derby which is used with the Hibernate configuration file.

In the `DAOImpl` class methods we are using `@preAuthorize` annotations.

Let's use the GlassFish application server to run the application.

Getting ready

▸ Edit the `application-security.xml`.

▸ Edit the `horrormovie-servlet.xml`.

▸ Use the `@preAuthorize` annotation in `DAOImpl`. Spring Security authorizes the user when the method is invoked.

How to do it...

The following steps will do authentication and authorization with a Hibernate application:

1. Edit the `application-security.xml` file with data source details and Bean information.

```
<global-method-security pre-post-annotations="enabled" />

  <http auto-config="false"  use-expressions="true">
```

```
      <intercept-url pattern="/login" access="permitAll" />
      <intercept-url pattern="/logout" access="permitAll" />
      <intercept-url pattern="/
        accessdenied" access="permitAll" />
      <intercept-url pattern="/**"
          access="hasRole('ROLE_EDITOR')" />
      <form-login login-page="/login" default-target-url=
        "/list" authentication-failure-url="/accessdenied" />
      <logout logout-success-url="/logout" />
  </http>

  <authentication-manager alias="authenticationManager">
    <authentication-provider>
      <jdbc-user-service data-source-ref="tenant1DataSource"
        users-by-username-query=" select username,password
        ,'true' as enabled from users where username=?"
        authorities-by-username-query="
        select u.username as username, ur.authority as
        authority from users u, user_roles ur
        where u.user_id = ur.user_id and u.username =?"
        />
    </authentication-provider>
  </authentication-manager>

  <beans:bean id="horrorMovieDAO" class=
    "com.packt.springsecurity.dao.HorrorMovieDaoImpl" />
  <beans:bean id="horrorMovieManager" class="com.packt.
    springsecurity.service.HorrorMovieManagerImpl" />
  <beans:bean id="tenant1DataSource" class=
    "org.springframework.jdbc.datasource.
    DriverManagerDataSource">
  <beans:property name="driverClassName" value=
    "org.apache.derby.jdbc.EmbeddedDriver" />
  <beans:property name="url" value=
    "jdbc:derby://localhost:1527/client1" />
  <beans:property name="username" value="client1" />
  <beans:property name="password" value="client1" />

</beans:bean>
```

2. Edit the `horrormovie-servlet.xml` file with the controller information.

```
<global-method-security pre-post-annotations="enabled" />

  <http auto-config="true">
    <intercept-url pattern=
      "/spring-security-wicket/**" access="ROLE_SELLER"/>
```

```
    <intercept-url pattern="/spring-security-wicket/*.*"
      access="ROLE_SELLER"/>
    <intercept-url pattern="/**" access="ROLE_SELLER" />
  <http-basic />
</http>
<authentication-manager>
  <authentication-provider>
    <jdbc-user-service data-source-ref="MySqlDS"
      users-by-username-query="
      select username,password, enabled
      from users1 where username=?"
      authorities-by-username-query="
      select u.username, ur.role from users1 u, user_roles ur
      where u.user_id = ur.user_id and u.username =?  " />
  </authentication-provider>
</authentication-manager>
```

It is using JDBC for authentication service.

3. Using the annotations when you execute the `addHorrorMovie` method Spring checks the security context object for credentials and does the authentication and authorization; this is given in the following code:

```
@Repository
public class HorrorMovieDaoImpl implements HorrorMovieDAO  {

  @Autowired
  private SessionFactory sessionFactory;

  @PreAuthorize("hasRole('ROLE_AUTHOR')")
  @Override
  public void addHorrorMovie(HorrorMovieEntity horrormovie)
  {
    this.sessionFactory.getCurrentSession()
      .save(horrormovie);
  }

  @SuppressWarnings("unchecked")
  @Override
  public List<HorrorMovieEntity> getAllHorrorMovies() {
    return this.sessionFactory.getCurrentSession()
      .createQuery("from HORRORMOVIE").list();
  }

  @Override
  public void deleteHorrorMovie(Integer horrorMovieId) {
```

```
        HorrorMovieEntity horrorMovie = (HorrorMovieEntity)
           sessionFactory.getCurrentSession()
          .load(HorrorMovieEntity.class, horrorMovieId);
      if (null != horrorMovie) {
        this.sessionFactory.getCurrentSession()
          .delete(horrorMovie);
      }
    }
  }
}
```

4. Some SQL commands are given as follows:

```
create table HORRORMOVIE
   (HORRORMOVIE_ID int generated by default as identity
     (START WITH 2, INCREMENT BY 1),
   HORRORMOVIE_NAME char(50),HORRORMOVIE_DIRECTOR char(50));


insert into HORRORMOVIE values
   (1, 'EVILDEAD','Fede Alvarez');
insert into HORRORMOVIE values
   (DEFAULT, 'EVILDEAD2','Fede Alvarez');
```

How it works...

In this example we have created a Hibernate application and used the JDBC service for authentication. The Spring framework interrupts the request to access the application and requests the user to enter the credentials. The credentials are authenticated using the JDBC details provided in the `application-security.xml` file.

On success the user is redirected to the application which displays a list of movies.

Now access the following URL:

```
http://localhost:8080/login
```

The screenshots for authenticating and authorizing using JDBC service and applying Spring Security on using annotation on methods are as follows:

The workflow of the example is shown in the following screenshots:

See also

- ▶ The *Spring Security with Hibernate using authentication provider* recipe
- ▶ The *Spring Security with Hibernate using user details service with Derby database* recipe
- ▶ The *Spring Security with MongoDB* recipe

Spring Security with Hibernate using authentication provider with @preAuthorize annotation

We are using the sample `horrormovie` application to demonstrate Spring Security with Hibernate using custom authentication provider and `@preAuthorize` annotation.

In this recipe we will create our own custom authentication provider and implement the interface authentication provider. We will apply the annotation on the `controller` method instead of the `hibernate` method.

Getting ready

- ▸ Create a new class which implements the `AuthenticationProvider` interface and add the Bean definition to the `application-security.xml` file

- ▸ Edit the `application-security.xml` file

- ▸ Use the `@preAuthorize` annotation in controller

How to do it...

The following steps are used to implement Spring Security by using the `AuthenticationProvider` interface:

1. Edit the `application-security.xml` file with data source details and Bean information.

   ```
   <global-method-security pre-post-annotations="enabled" />

   <http auto-config="false"  use-expressions="true">
     <intercept-url pattern="/login" access="permitAll" />
     <intercept-url pattern="/logout" access="permitAll" />
     <intercept-url pattern="/accessdenied" access="permitAll"
       />
     <intercept-url pattern="/list" access=
       "hasRole('ROLE_EDITOR')" />
     <intercept-url pattern="/add" access=
       "hasRole('ROLE_EDITOR')" />
     <form-login login-page="/login" default-target-url
       ="/list" authentication-failure-url="/accessdenied" />
     <logout logout-success-url="/logout" />
   </http>
   ```

```xml
<authentication-manager alias="authenticationManager">
<authentication-provider ref=
  "MyCustomAuthenticationProvider" />
</authentication-manager>

<beans:bean id="horrorMovieDAO" class=
  "com.packt.springsecurity.dao.HorrorMovieDaoImpl" />
<beans:bean id="horrorMovieManager" class=
  "com.packt.springsecurity.service.HorrorMovieManagerImpl"
  />

<beans:bean id="MyCustomAuthenticationProvider" class=
  "com.packt.springsecurity.controller" />
</beans:beans>
```

2. Edit the `MyCustomAuthenticationProvider` file.

```java
public class MyCustomAuthenticationProvider
  implements AuthenticationProvider {
  @Override
  public boolean supports(Class<? extends Object>
    authentication)
{
    return (UsernamePasswordAuthenticationToken.
      class.isAssignableFrom(authentication));
    }

  private static Map<String, String> APP_USERS
    = new HashMap<String, String>(2);
  private static List<GrantedAuthority> APP_ROLES
    = new ArrayList<GrantedAuthority>();
  static
  {
    APP_USERS.put("ravi", "ravi123");
    APP_USERS.put("chitra", "chitra123");
    APP_ROLES.add(new SimpleGrantedAuthority("ROLE_EDITOR"));
  }

  @Override
  public Authentication authenticate(Authentication auth)
  {
    if (APP_USERS.containsKey(auth.getPrincipal())
    && APP_ROLES.get(auth.getPrincipal())
      .equals(auth.getCredentials()))
    {
      return new UsernamePasswordAuthenticationToken
        (auth.getName(), auth.getCredentials(),
```

```
        AUTHORITIES);
    }
    throw new BadCredentialsException("Username/Password
        does not match for "
      + auth.getPrincipal());
    }
  }
}
```

3. Use the annotations in controller.

```
AddHorrorMovieController
@PreAuthorize("hasRole('ROLE_EDITOR')")
@RequestMapping(value = "/add", method = RequestMethod.POST)
public String addHorrorMovie(
  @ModelAttribute(value = "horrorMovie") HorrorMovieEntity
    horrorMovie,
    BindingResult result) {
    horrorMovieManager.addHorrorMovie(horrorMovie);
    return "redirect:/list";
  }
```

How it works...

Now access the following URL:

```
http://localhost:8080/login
```

After interrupting the request, Spring Security invokes `MyCustomAuthenticationProvider`, which has the overridden authenticate method for authentication and also the user information. The user credentials are authenticated and authorized with the credentials in `APP_Users` map on successful authentication and authorization the user will be redirected to the success URL configured in the `spring-security.xml` file.

The screenshots for authenticating and authorizing using the custom authentication provider and applying Spring Security on using annotation on methods in the controller are as follows:

See also

- ► The *Spring Security with Hibernate using @preAuthorize annotation* recipe
- ► The *Spring Security with Hibernate using custom authentication provider with @preAuthorize annotation* recipe
- ► The *Spring Security with Hibernate using user details service with Derby database* recipe
- ► The *Spring Security with MongoDB* recipe

Spring Security with Hibernate using UserDetailsService with Derby database

So far we have seen Hibernate and Spring security with various authentication providers. In this section we will use Hibernate to retrieve users and authorities from the database.

For that we are going to implement the UserDetailsService interface and implement a method in the interface. To begin we need to create entity classes for users and roles.

We also moved the @preAuthorize annotation to the controller class.

Getting ready

> ▸ Create a new class which implements the UserDetailsService interface and add the Bean definition to the application-security.xml file

> ▸ Edit the application-security.xml file

> ▸ Use the @preAuthorize annotation in controller

> ▸ In the horror database add the tables USERS and USER_ROLE

> ▸ Insert role ROLE_EDITOR and users named ravi and ravi123

How to do it...

The following steps are used to integrate Spring Security authentication with Hibernate by implementing the UserDetailsService interface that interacts with Hibernate methods:

1. Create a class MyUserDetailsService which implements the UserDetailsService interface.

```
public class MyUserDetails implements UserDetailsService {
  @Autowired
  private UsersDAO UsersDAO;
  public UserDetails loadUserByUsername(String userName)
  throws UsernameNotFoundException {

    Users users= UsersDAO.findByUserName(userName);
    boolean enabled = true;
    boolean accountNonExpired = true;
    boolean credentialsNonExpired = true;
    boolean accountNonLocked = true;
    return new User(
      users.getUserName(),
      users.getUserPassword(),
```

```
      enabled,
      accountNonExpired,
      credentialsNonExpired,
      accountNonLocked,
      getAuthorities(users.getRole()
        .getRoleId().intValue()));
    }


  public Collection<? extends GrantedAuthority>
      getAuthorities(Integer role) {
    List<GrantedAuthority> authList =
      getGrantedAuthorities(getRoles(role));
    System.out.println("authList----------->"+authList);
    return authList;
  }


  public List<String> getRoles(Integer role) {

    List<String> roles = new ArrayList<String>();

    if (role.intValue() == 1) {
      roles.add("ROLE_EDITOR");
    } else if (role.intValue() == 2) {
      roles.add("ROLE_AUTHOR");
    }
    return roles;
  }


  public static List<GrantedAuthority>
    getGrantedAuthorities(List<String> roles) {
    List<GrantedAuthority> authorities = new
      ArrayList<GrantedAuthority>();
    for (String role : roles) {
      System.out.println("role----------->"+role);
      authorities.add(new SimpleGrantedAuthority(role));
    }
    return authorities;
  }


}
```

2. Edit the `application-security.xml` file.

```
<authentication-manager alias="authenticationManager">
  <authentication-provider user-service-ref="MyUserDetails">
    <password-encoder hash="plaintext" />
```

```
      </authentication-provider>
    </authentication-manager>


    <beans:bean id="horrorMovieDAO" class=
      "com.packt.springsecurity.dao.HorrorMovieDaoImpl" />
    <beans:bean id="horrorMovieManager" class="com.
      packt.springsecurity.service.HorrorMovieManagerImpl" />
    <beans:bean id="UsersDAO" class=
      "com.packt.springsecurity.dao.UsersDAOImpl" />
    <beans:bean id="UsersManager" class=
      "com.packt.springsecurity.service.UsersManagerImpl" />
    <beans:bean id="UserRoleDAO" class=
      "com.packt.springsecurity.dao.UserRoleDAOImpl" />
    <beans:bean id="UserRoleManager" class=
      "com.packt.springsecurity.service.UserRoleManagerImpl" />


    <beans:bean id="MyUserDetails" class=
      "com.packt.springsecurity.service.MyUserDetails" />
    </beans:beans>
```

3. Use annotations in controller.

```
@PreAuthorize("hasRole('ROLE_EDITOR')")
@RequestMapping(value = "/add", method = RequestMethod.POST)
public String addHorrorMovie(
  @ModelAttribute(value = "horrorMovie")
    HorrorMovieEntity horrorMovie,
  BindingResult result) {
    horrorMovieManager.addHorrorMovie(horrorMovie);
    return "redirect:/list";
}
```

How it works...

Now access the following URL:

`http://localhost:8080/login`

First we authenticate and authorize using UserDetailsService and Hibernate. UserDetailsService is a Spring Security interface which is implemented by MyUserDetailsService class. This class is configured in the application-security. xml file so that Spring Security invokes this implementation class to load the user details using Hibernate. UsersDAO.findByUserName(userName) is a method to invoke Hibernate to get the user information based on the username that is passed.

After applying Spring Security to the controller using annotations, we should be able to login with the username and password (ravi and ravi123). The `<password-encoder hash="plaintext" />` is a hashing algorithm supported by Spring Security. On successful authentication the user will be redirected to the authorized page.

The workflow of the application is demonstrated in the following screenshots:

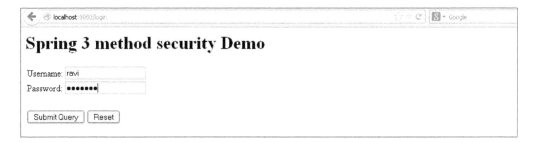

See also

- The *Spring Security with Hibernate using @preAuthorize annotation* recipe
- The *Spring Security with Hibernate using custom authentication provider with @preAuthorize annotation* recipe
- The *Spring Security with Hibernate using user details service with Derby database* recipe
- The *Spring Security with MongoDB* recipe

Spring Security with MongoDB

In this section let's see how Spring Security works with MongoDB. MongoDB is a popular NOSQL database. It is a document based database. MongoDB is written in the popular C++ database which makes it an object oriented document based database. In MongoDB queries are also document based, and it also provides indexing using JSON style to store and retrieve data. The latest Spring version available is Version 3.2 has been included in the POC.

Getting ready

- Download the MongoDB database
- Configure the data folder
- Start MongoDB in command prompt
- Start MongoDB in another command prompt
- Create `horrordb` database by inserting data into it
- Execute the command `use horrordb`
- Add MongoDB dependency to the **POM** (**Project Object Model**) file
- Add JSON dependency to the POM file
- Upgrade the Spring Version to 3.2.0 and Spring Security to 1.4
- Create a `MongoUserDetails` class
- Edit the `horror-movie` servlet
- Edit the `Application-security.xml` file

How to do it...

The following steps use Mongo with Spring Security to authenticate and authorize users by implementing the `UserDetailsService` interface:

1. Database operations in command prompt is shown as follows:

```
db.horrormovie.insert({horrormovie_id:1,horrormovie_name:
  "omen",horrormovie_director:"Richard Donner"})


db.horrormovie.insert({horrormovie_id:2,horrormovie_name:
  "the conjuring",horrormovie_director:"James Wan"})


db.horrormovie.insert({horrormovie_id:3,horrormovie_name:
  "The Lords of Salem",horrormovie_director:"Rob Zombie"})
```

```
db.horrormovie.insert({horrormovie_id:4,horrormovie_name:
  "Evil Dead",horrormovie_director: "Fede Alvarez"})

db.users.insert({id:1,username:"anjana",password:
  "123456",role:1})

db.users.insert({id:2,username:"raghu",password:
  "123456",role:2})

db.users.insert({id:3,username:"shami",password:
  "123456",role:3})
```

2. Create a class `MongoUserDetailsService` which implements the `UserDetailsService` interface.

```
@Service
public class MongoUserDetailsService implements
  UserDetailsService {

  @Autowired
  private UserManager userManager;
  private static final Logger logger =
    Logger.getLogger(MongoUserDetailsService.class);
  private org.springframework.security.
    core.userdetails.User userdetails;
  public UserDetails loadUserByUsername(String username)
  throws UsernameNotFoundException {
    boolean enabled = true;
    boolean accountNonExpired = true;
    boolean credentialsNonExpired = true;
    boolean accountNonLocked = true;
    Users users = getUserDetail(username);
    System.out.println(username);
    System.out.println(users.getPassword());
    System.out.println(users.getUsername());
    System.out.println(users.getRole());

    return new User(users.getUsername(),
      users.getPassword()
      ,enabled,accountNonExpired,credentialsNonExpired,
      accountNonLocked,getAuthorities(users.getRole()));
  }
```

```java
    public List<GrantedAuthority> getAuthorities(Integer
      role) {
      List<GrantedAuthority> authList =
        new ArrayList<GrantedAuthority>();
        if (role.intValue() == 1) {
          authList.add(new SimpleGrantedAuthority
            ("ROLE_EDITOR"));

        } else if (role.intValue() == 2) {
          authList.add(new SimpleGrantedAuthority
            ("ROLE_AUTHOR"));
      }
      return authList;
    }

    public Users getUserDetail(String username) {
    Users users = userManager.findByUserName(username);
    System.out.println(users.toString());
    return users;
    }
```

3. Edit the `application-security.xml`.

```xml
<global-method-security pre-post-annotations="enabled" />

<http auto-config="false"  use-expressions="true">
  <intercept-url pattern="/login" access="permitAll" />
  <intercept-url pattern="/logout" access="permitAll" />
  <intercept-url pattern="/accessdenied" access=
    "permitAll" />
  <intercept-url pattern="/list"
    access="hasRole('ROLE_EDITOR')" />
<!--                  <http-basic/>-->
  <form-login login-page="/login" default-target-url=
    "/list" authentication-failure-url="/accessdenied" />
  <logout logout-success-url="/logout" />
</http>

<authentication-manager alias="authenticationManager">
<authentication-provider user-service-ref=
  "mongoUserDetailsService">
<password-encoder hash="plaintext" />
</authentication-provider>
</authentication-manager>
```

4. Edit the `horrormovie-servlet.xml`.

```xml
<context:annotation-config />
<context:component-scan base-package=
  "com.packt.springsecurity.mongodb.controller" />
<context:component-scan base-package=
  "com.packt.springsecurity.mongodb.manager" />
<context:component-scan base-package=
  "com.packt.springsecurity.mongodb.dao" />
<context:component-scan base-package=
  "com.packt.springsecurity.mongodb.documententity" />

<bean id="jspViewResolver"
  class="org.springframework.web.servlet
  .view.InternalResourceViewResolver">
  <property name="viewClass"
  value="org.springframework.web.servlet.view.JstlView" />
  <property name="prefix" value="/WEB-INF/view/" />
  <property name="suffix" value=".jsp" />
</bean>
<mongo:mongo host="127.0.0.1" port="27017" />
<mongo:db-factory dbname="horrordb" />

<bean id="mongoTemplate" class=
  "org.springframework.data.mongodb.core.MongoTemplate">
<constructor-arg name="mongoDbFactory" ref=
  "mongoDbFactory" />
</bean>

<bean id="horrorMovieDAO" class="com.packt.
  springsecurity.mongodb.dao.HorrorMovieDaoImpl" />
<bean id="horrorMovieManager" class="com.packt.
  springsecurity.mongodb.manager.HorrorMovieManagerImpl" />
<bean id="UsersDAO" class="com.packt.
  springsecurity.mongodb.dao.UsersDAOImpl" />
<bean id="userManager" class="com.packt.
  springsecurity.mongodb.manager.UserManagerImpl" />
<bean id="mongoUserDetailsService" class="com.
  packt.springsecurity.mongodb.controller.
  MongoUserDetailsService" />

<bean id="HorroMovieController" class="com.packt.
  springsecurity.mongodb.controller.HorrorMovieController"
  />
```

5. Use the annotations in controller.

```
@PreAuthorize("hasRole('ROLE_EDITOR')")
@RequestMapping(value = "/add", method = RequestMethod.POST)
public String addHorrorMovie(
@ModelAttribute(value = "horrorMovie")
  HorrorMovieEntity horrorMovie,
 BindingResult result) {
 horrorMovieManager.addHorrorMovie(horrorMovie);
 return "redirect:/list";
}
```

How it works...

First we authenticate and authorize using MongoDetailsService and Spring data. MongoDetailsService is the implementation of UserDetailsService, getUserDetail(string username) invokes the springdata classes to get user credentials from the Mongo database based on the username passed. If the data is present based on the username, it implies that the authentication is successful. We then apply Spring Security on the controller methods using annotation.

Now we should be able to login with the username and password (ravi and 123456).

Now access the following URL:

http://localhost:8080/login

The workflow is demonstrated in the following screenshots:

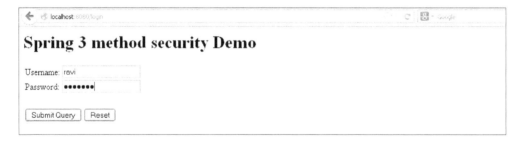

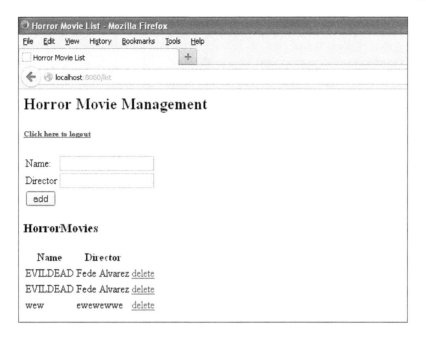

See also

- ▸ The *Spring Security with Hibernate using @preAuthorize annotation* recipe
- ▸ The *Spring Security with Hibernate using custom authentication provider with @preAuthorize annotation* recipe
- ▸ The *Spring Security with Hibernate using user details service with Derby database* recipe
- ▸ The *Spring Security with MongoDB* recipe

9
Spring Security with Spring Social

In this chapter we will cover:

- ► Spring Security with Spring Social to access Facebook
- ► Spring Security with Spring Social to access Twitter
- ► Spring Security with multiple authentication providers
- ► Spring Security with OAuth

Introduction

Spring Social is a famous API. Most web applications want to give users an option to post to social networking sites such as Facebook and Twitter from their application. Spring Social is built to meet this requirement.

In this chapter, we shall integrate Spring Security with Spring Social to connect to Facebook and Twitter accounts.

Spring Security with Spring Social to access Facebook

For authentication, Spring Social uses the `spring-security` API. We need to add the spring-social dependency in the `pom.xml` along with with the `spring-core` and `spring-security` packages. In this section we shall demonstrate how Spring Social can bridge our java application to Facebook. We can log in to the Facebook application in our java application.

Once the connection is established to the social networking site, the user can post and retrieve messages from it.

We have used the same hibernate horror movie application. I have used derby database and have deployed the application on the glassfish server. Spring Social internally uses Spring's `jdbctemplate` class to retrieve database information.

Getting ready

You will need to perform the following tasks to access Facebook using Spring Security with Spring Social:

▸ Register as a Facebook developer and create an app. You will get an appID and secret key which can be used for integration

▸ Add request mapping to the controller to handle the Facebook created `jsp` pages to post messages onto Facebook

▸ Create the `UserConnection` table

▸ Add Jackson dependency into your `pom.xml` file. The demo project will be available for download with this book

▸ Add the Spring Social dependencies such as:

  ❑ `Spring-social-core`

  ❑ `Spring-social-web`

  ❑ `Spring-social-facebook`

  ❑ `Spring-social-twitter`

  ❑ `Spring-social-linkedin`

  ❑ `Spring-social-github`

▸ Create the `.jsp` pages for the user to sign in and sign out

▸ Provide the database connection properties in the `spring.properties` file

▸ Provide Facebook's apps- secret key and appID in the `jdbc.properties` file

How to do it...

The following are the steps for implementing an application that allow users to sign in to the Facebook app with Spring Social and Spring Security:

1. Create a controller named `MyController` to handle the Facebook pages.

```
@RequestMapping(value = "/fbprofile", method =
  RequestMethod.GET)
public String getfbProfile(ModelMap model,
  HttpServletRequest request,
```

```
        HttpServletResponse response) {
    model.addAttribute("request.userPrincipal.name",
      request.getUserPrincipal().getName());
    Facebook facebook = connectionRepository.
      getPrimaryConnection(Facebook.class).getApi();
    model.addAttribute("profileLink", facebook.
      userOperations().getUserProfile().getLink());
    model.addAttribute("Gender", facebook.userOperations().
      getUserProfile().getGender());
    model.addAttribute("profileInfo", facebook.
      userOperations().getUserProfile());
    model.addAttribute("userpermissions", facebook.
      userOperations().getUserPermissions());
    List<Reference> friends = facebook.
      friendOperations().getFriends();
    model.addAttribute("friends", friends);
    model.addAttribute("friendlist", facebook.
      friendOperations().getFriendLists());
    return "facebookprofile";
}
```

2. Provide the connection factories in the `Spring-social.xml` file:

```xml
<bean id="connectionFactoryLocator"
  class="org.springframework.social.connect.support.
  ConnectionFactoryRegistry">
  <property name="connectionFactories">
    <list>
      <bean class="org.springframework.social.
        facebook.connect.FacebookConnectionFactory">
        <constructor-arg value="${facebook.clientId}" />
        <constructor-arg value="${facebook.clientSecret}"
          />
      </bean>
    </list>
  </property>
</bean>
```

The `ConnectionFactory` locator creates the Facebook bean. Here you can add other social networking providers such as Digg and Flickr. `UsersConnectionRepository` uses the JDBC template to execute queries for connecting with various social networking providers.

3. Use the connection factory in the `spring-social.xml` file:

```xml
<bean id="textEncryptor" class="org.springframework.
  security.crypto.encrypt.Encryptors"
    factory-method="noOpText" />
<bean id="usersConnectionRepository" class="org.
  springframework.social.connect.jdbc.
    JdbcUsersConnectionRepository">
  <constructor-arg ref="mydataSource" />
  <constructor-arg ref="connectionFactoryLocator" />
  <constructor-arg ref="textEncryptor" />
</bean>
<bean id="connectionRepository" factory-
  method="createConnectionRepository"
    factory-bean="usersConnectionRepository"
      scope="request">
  <constructor-arg
    value="#{request.userPrincipal.name}" />
  <aop:scoped-proxy proxy-target-class="false"/>
</bean>
```

4. Configure the `ConnectController` class in the `spring-social` file. The `ConnectController` class plays an important role in connecting to the provider. It is mapped with the (`/connect`) URL. To make best use of the `ConnectController` class, create separate folders for Facebook and Twitter.

```xml
<bean class="org.springframework.
  social.connect.web.ConnectController"
  p:applicationUrl="${application.url}"/>
```

5. Run a SQL command in your derby database.

```sql
create table UserConnection (userId varchar(255) not null,
  providerId varchar(255) not null,
  providerUserId varchar(255),
  rank int not null,
  displayName varchar(255),
  profileUrl varchar(512),
  imageUrl varchar(512),
  accessToken varchar(255) not null,
  secret varchar(255),
  refreshToken varchar(255),
  expireTime bigint,
  primary key (userId, providerId, providerUserId));

create unique index UserConnectionRank on
  UserConnection(userId, providerId, rank);
```

How it works...

Spring Social uses the `UserConnection` table to store the networking site provider information along with the user information. Spring Social uses Spring Security along with the appID and secret key to authenticate the user.

Access the URL: `http://localhost:8080/horrormovie/list`

You will be redirected to `http://localhost:8080/horrormovie/login;jsessionid=581813e14c1752d2260521830d3d`.

Log in with the username and password. You will be connected to the `horromovie` database, as shown in the following screenshot:

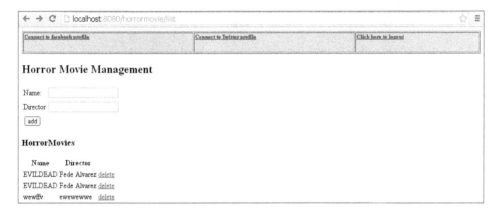

Click on the **Connect to Facebook profile** link, and the user will be redirected to the following web page:

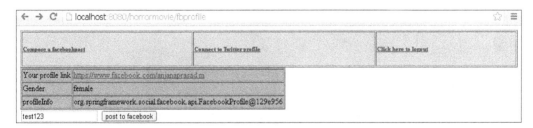

The page displays the following fields:

- ▸ Profile link
- ▸ Gender
- ▸ Profile info
- ▸ Textbox to post messages to Facebook

You can post messages from this application and then open the Facebook profile to see the posted messages. The message will be posted in the name of the Facebook app that you have created.

See also

▶ The *Spring Security with Spring Social to access Twitter* recipe

▶ The *Spring Security with multiple authentication providers* recipe

▶ The *Spring Security with OAuth* recipe

Spring Security with Spring Social to access Twitter

We just now connected with Facebook and were able to post messages. In this section, we will see how to connect to Twitter. Let's use the same application that we used for Facebook with derby database and hibernate the authentication service.

Getting ready

You will need to perform the following tasks to access Twitter with Spring Social using Spring Security:

▶ Create a Twitter app: `https://dev.twitter.com/apps/new`

▶ Add the consumer ID and key to the `.properties` file.

▶ Update the controller to handle Twitter requests

▶ Create JSP files to access and display Twitter objects

How to do it...

The following is the step for implementing Twitter sign-in options in the application demonstrated in the previous section:

1. Update the controller named `HorrorMovie Controller` to handle Twitter requests.

```
< @RequestMapping(value = "/posttofb", method =
  RequestMethod.GET)
  public String posttofb(String message, ModelMap model) {
    try {
      Facebook facebook = connectionRepository.
        getPrimaryConnection(Facebook.class).getApi();
      facebook.feedOperations().updateStatus(message);
      model.addAttribute("status", "success");
```

```java
        model.addAttribute("message", message);
        return "redirect:/list";
      } catch (Exception e) {
        model.addAttribute("status", "failure");
        return "/facebook/fbconnect";
      }
    }
    @RequestMapping(value = "/twprofile", method =
      RequestMethod.GET)
    public String gettwProfile(ModelMap model) {
      try{
        Twitter twitter = connectionRepository.
          getPrimaryConnection(Twitter.class).getApi();
        model.addAttribute("twprofileLink",
          twitter.userOperations().
            getUserProfile().getUrl());
        model.addAttribute("twprofileInfo",
          twitter.userOperations().getUserProfile());
        model.addAttribute("twfollowers",
          twitter.friendOperations().getFollowers());
        model.addAttribute("twfriends",
          twitter.friendOperations().getFriends());
        return "/twitter/twitterprofile";
      } catch (Exception e) {
        model.addAttribute("status", "failure");
        return "/twitter/twconnect";
      }
    }
    @RequestMapping(value = "/posttotw", method =
      RequestMethod.GET)
    public String posttotw(String message, ModelMap model) {
      try {
        Twitter twitter = connectionRepository.
          getPrimaryConnection(Twitter.class).getApi();
        twitter.timelineOperations().updateStatus(message);
        model.addAttribute("status", "success");
        model.addAttribute("message", message);
        return "redirect:/list";
      } catch (Exception e) {
        model.addAttribute("status", "failure");
        return "/twitter/twconnect";
      }
    }
```

How it works...

Access the URL: `http://localhost:8080/horrormovie/list`.

Spring Social will check if the user is already connected to Twitter. If the user is already connected, the user is redirected to Twitter page and will be asked to log in. Spring Social uses the Twitter consumer ID and key with Spring Security to log in to Twitter account from the application. This is the basis on which most of the mobile phone applications allow us to log in to Twitter and Facebook.

See also

- The *Spring Security with Spring Social to access Facebook* recipe
- The *Spring Security with multiple authentication providers* recipe
- The *Spring Security with OAuth* recipe

Spring Security with multiple authentication providers

In this section, we will demonstrate multiple authentications with Spring Social and database. In our previous recipe, we used the `ConnectController` class which handled the Facebook and Twitter connections. Access to Facebook and Twitter was restricted to the Spring Security URL, that is, only `ROLE_EDITOR` had access to Facebook and Twitter. The user had to be authenticated and authorized to use Facebook and Twitter. In this example, we shall allow the users to log in to the application with Facebook and Twitter or normal user ID.

Craig Walls is a lead on Spring Social API and has provided various samples on gitHub, which uses Spring Social with Spring Security. This is one of the samples provided by *Craig Walls*.

Getting ready

You will need to perform the following tasks:

1. Create a common page to sign in as a user or sign up using Twitter, Facebook, or linked-in profiles.

2. Spring Social API has a `ConnectController` class, which automatically looks out for a connect folder. Create a connect folder, add `${provider}Connect.jsp` and `${provider} Connected.jsp`. `$provider{twitter,facebook,linked-in,github}`

3. Spring Social internally uses `spring-security`. It has its own user details class – `SocialUserDetailsService`. Create a class that implements `SocialUserDetailsService` and override the method.

4. Configure the social authentication provider in the `social-security.xml` file. The `SocialAuthenticationProvider` class accepts two inputs such as:

   ❑ `usersConnectionRepository`

   ❑ `socialuserDetailsService` – the class that implements `SocialUserDetailsService`

5. Configure the multiple authentication providers in `security-xml`:

   ❑ `SocialAuthenticationProvider`

   ❑ `UserDetailsService`, the jdbc interface giving user details service

6. Configuring the filter, `SocialAuthenticationFilter`, for handling the provider sign-in flow within the Spring Security filter chain. It should be added into the chain at or before the `PRE_AUTH_FILTER` location.

How to do it...

The following are the steps to implement authentication with multiple providers using Spring Security:

1. Use the `SocialUsersDetailServiceImpl` class to implement the `SocialUserDetailsService` class:

```
public class SocialUsersDetailServiceImpl implements
SocialUserDetailsService {
  private UserDetailsService userDetailsService;
  public SocialUsersDetailServiceImpl(UserDetailsService
    userDetailsService) {
    this.userDetailsService = userDetailsService;
  }
  @Override
    public SocialUserDetails loadUserByUserId(String
      userId) throws UsernameNotFoundException,
        DataAccessException {
    UserDetails userDetails = userDetailsService.
      loadUserByUsername(userId);
    return new SocialUser(userDetails.getUsername(),
      userDetails.getPassword(),
        userDetails.getAuthorities());
}}
```

2. Configure the class, `SocialAuthenticationProvider` in the `Security.xml` file:

```
<bean id="socialAuthenticationProvider"
  class="org.springframework.social.
  security.SocialAuthenticationProvider"
  c:_0-ref="usersConnectionRepository"
  c:_1-ref="socialUsersDetailService" />
<bean id="socialUsersDetailService"
  class="org.springframework.social.
  showcase.security.SocialUsersDetailServiceImpl"
  c:_-ref="userDetailsService" />
```

3. Configure multiple authentication providers in the `Security.xml` file:

```
<authentication-manager alias="authenticationManager">
  <authentication-provider user-service-
    ref="userDetailsService">
    <password-encoder ref="passwordEncoder" />
  </authentication-provider>
  <!-- Spring Social Security authentication provider -->
  <authentication-provider
    ref="socialAuthenticationProvider" />
</authentication-manager>
<jdbc-user-service id="userDetailsService"
  data-source-ref="dataSource"
    users-by-username-query="select username, password,
      true from Account where username = ?"
    authorities-by-username-query="select username,
      'ROLE_USER' from Account where username = ?"/>
<beans:bean id="textEncryptor"
  class="org.springframework.security.
    crypto.encrypt.Encryptors"
  factory-method="noOpText" />
<beans:bean id="passwordEncoder"
  class="org.springframework.security.
    crypto.password.NoOpPasswordEncoder"
  factory-method="getInstance" />
```

4. Configure the `SocialAuthenticationFilter` class in the `Social-security.xml` file:

```
<bean id="socialAuthenticationFilter" class="org.springframework.
social.security.SocialAuthenticationFilter"
    c:_0-ref="authenticationManager"
    c:_1-ref="userIdSource"
    c:_2-ref="usersConnectionRepository"
    c:_3-ref="connectionFactoryLocator"
    p:signupUrl="/spring-social-showcase/signup"
```

```
p:rememberMeServices-ref="org.springframework.
    security.web.authentication.rememberme.
        TokenBasedRememberMeServices#0" />
```

5. Configure the `SocialAuthenticationFilter` class with Security in the `security.xml` file:

```xml
<http use-expressions="true">
    <!-- Authentication policy -->
    <form-login login-page="/signin" login-processing-
        url="/signin/authenticate" authentication-failure-
            url="/signin?param.error=bad_credentials" />
    <logout logout-url="/signout" delete-
        cookies="JSESSIONID" />
    <intercept-url pattern="/favicon.ico"
        access="permitAll" />
    <intercept-url pattern="/resources/**"
        access="permitAll" />
    <intercept-url pattern="/auth/**" access="permitAll" />
    <intercept-url pattern="/signin/**" access="permitAll"
        />
    <intercept-url pattern="/signup/**" access="permitAll"
        />
    <intercept-url pattern="/disconnect/facebook"
        access="permitAll" />
    <intercept-url pattern="/**" access="isAuthenticated()"
        />
    <remember-me />
    <!-- Spring Social Security authentication filter -->
    <custom-filter ref="socialAuthenticationFilter"
        before="PRE_AUTH_FILTER" />
</http>
```

How it works...

In this implementation, the user can log in to the application either by using some credentials in the database or by using the social networking site ID and password. The `SocialAuthenticationProvider` class along with `SocialAuthenticationFilter` handles the authentication to social networking sites and `UserDetailsService` manages the database authentication. These two classes are configured in the `security.xml` file.

The following is the workflow of the implementation. Access the URL: `http://localhost:8080/spring-social-showcase-sec-xml/signin`. You will be directed to the following web page:

See also

▸ The *Spring Security with Spring Social to access Facebook* recipe

▸ The *Spring Security with Spring Social to access Twitter* recipe

▸ The *Spring Security with OAuth* recipe

Spring Security with OAuth

OAuth authentication has been used widely by many applications. OAuth is a protocol through which applications can share the data in a secured manner. For example, consider a simple scenario in which one photo-sharing application allows the user to upload photos and the second application integrates with all photo-storing applications such as Flickr, Dropbox, and similar sites. When a second application wants to access the first application to print the photos that are uploaded, it uses the OAuth authentication to get confirmation from the user to access the photos. Ideally, it does exchange some security tokens between the applications, that is, the private key of the consumer and the public key of the server should match for the authorization to be successful.

The first application acts likes a server and the second application acts like a consumer who wants to access certain authenticated data.

Some of the parameters that are exchanged between the client and server applications are as follows:

- ▸ `Oauth_consumerKey`: We can generate an OAuth request using the application
- ▸ `Oauth_token`: This token gets encoded and is passed to the URL
- ▸ `Oauth_timestamp`: This parameter is added to each request with nonce to prevent the serviced request being used again called as replay attacks
- ▸ `Oauth_version`: This defines the version of OAuth protocol being used
- ▸ `Oauth_signaturemethod`: This parameter is used to sign and verify the request
- ▸ `Oauth_nonce`: This parameter is used with timestamp
- ▸ `Size`: This parameter defines the size of the file
- ▸ `File`: This parameter defines the name of the file

Let's develop a sample client-server application to demonstrate OAuth with Spring Security:

- ▸ The server application: Let's think of a movie story application. The application accepts stories from the users. The users can upload their stories to the application. This application behaves like a service provider. A user writes some horror stories and submits them to movie making companies.
- ▸ The client application: Think of another movie making company application that accepts stories to be uploaded from the server application. The movie making company has to get authorization from the movie story application to download the stories.

Getting ready

Perform the following tasks to integrate Spring Security with OAuth:

- ▸ Create a server application with the `ConfirmAccessController` and `StoryController` classes
- ▸ Create a client-side application to access server data
- ▸ Add `spring-security-oauth` dependency to the `pom.xml` file

How to do it...

The following are the steps to integrate `spring-security` with `spring-oauth`:

1. Create the `CreateStoryController` class for stories.

```
@Controller
public class CreateStoryController {
  @RequestMapping(value="/stories",
    method=RequestMethod.GET)
```

```java
@ResponseBody
public String loadStory() {
  StringBuilder horrorStory = new StringBuilder();
  horrorStory.append("Story Name -- Conjuring:
    Author").append(getAuthorName()).append(" Story:She
    and that girl and occasionally another girl went out
    several times a week, and the rest of the time Connie
    spent around the house—it was summer vacation—getting
    in her mother's way and thinking, dreaming about the
    boys she met. But all the boys fell back and
    dissolved into a single face that was not even a face
    but an idea, a feeling, mixed up with the urgent
    insistent pounding of the music and the humid night
    air of July. Connie's mother kept dragging her back
    to the daylight by finding things for her to do or
    saying suddenly, 'What's this about the Pettinger
    girl?");
  return horrorStory.toString();
}
private String getAuthorName() {
  Object principal = SecurityContextHolder.
    getContext().getAuthentication().getPrincipal();
  String author;
  if (principal instanceof UserDetails) {
    author = ((UserDetails)principal).getUsername();
  } else {
    author = principal.toString();
  }
  return author;
}
}
```

2. Create the `ConfirmAccessController` class.

```java
@Controller
public class ConfirmAccessController {
  private ClientAuthenticationCache
    clientauthenticationCache = new
      DefaultClientAuthenticationCache();
  private ClientDetailsService clientDetailsService;
  public ClientAuthenticationCache getAuthenticationCache() {
    return clientauthenticationCache;
  }
  @RequestMapping(value="/oauth/confirm_access")
  public ModelAndView accessConfirmation(HttpServletRequest
    request, HttpServletResponse response) {
```

```java
      ClientAuthenticationToken clientAuthtoken =
   getAuthenticationCache().getAuthentication(request, response);
      if (clientAuthtoken == null) {
        throw new IllegalStateException("We did not recive
          any client authentication to authorize");
      }
      ClientDetails client = getClientDetailsService().
        loadClientByClientId(clientAuthtoken.getClientId());
      TreeMap<String, Object> model = new TreeMap<String,
        Object>();
      model.put("auth_request", clientAuthtoken);
      model.put("client", client);
      return new ModelAndView("access_confirmation", model);
    }
    public ClientDetailsService getClientDetailsService() {
      return clientDetailsService;
    }
    @Autowired
    public void setClientDetailsService(
        ClientDetailsService clientDetailsService) {
      this.clientDetailsService = clientDetailsService;
    }
  }
```

3. Configure Spring Security with OAuth.

```xml
<!-- Root Context: defines shared resources visible to all other
web components -->
  <http auto-config='true'>
  <intercept-url pattern="/**" access="ROLE_EDITOR" />
  </http>
  <authentication-manager>
    <authentication-provider>
      <user-service>
        <user name="anju" password="anju123"
          authorities="ROLE_EDITOR" />
      </user-service>
    </authentication-provider>
  </authentication-manager>
  <!--apply the oauth client context -->
  <oauth:client token-services-ref="oauth2TokenServices" />
  <beans:bean id="oauth2TokenServices"
  class="org.springframework.security.oauth2.
    consumer.token.InMemoryOAuth2ClientTokenServices" />
  <oauth:resource id="story" type="authorization_code"
```

```
      clientId="movie" accessTokenUri="
        http://localhost:8080/story/oauth/authorize"
      userAuthorizationUri="
        http://localhost:8080/story/oauth/user/authorize" />
      <beans:bean id="storyService"
        class="org.springsource.oauth.StoryServiceImpl">
      <beans:property name="storyURL" value="
        http://localhost:8080/story/stories"></beans:property>
      <beans:property name="storyRestTemplate">
        <beans:bean class="org.springframework.
          security.oauth2.consumer.OAuth2RestTemplate">
        <beans:constructor-arg ref="story"/>
        </beans:bean>
      </beans:property>
      <beans:property name="tokenServices"
        ref="oauth2TokenServices"></beans:property>
    </beans:bean>
  </beans:beans>
```

How it works...

You have to first access the `movieCompanyapp` site. The `movieCompanyapp` in turn gets stories from the `storyapp` site. So we have to deploy both the applications in the same port.

We created two users (`raghu/raghu123` for `movieCompanyapp` and `anju/anju123` for `storyapp`). When the user clicks on the **Get stories from storyapp** link, the user will be asked to log in again. This time the user has to enter their credentials, and then they will get to read the story.

Access the URL: `http://localhost:8080/movieCompanyapp/spring_security_log in;jsessionid=3b654cf3917d105caa7c273283b5`

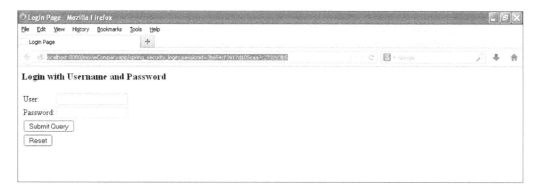

You will be asked to authorize in order to show the story to the company. This happens in the `storyapp` application.

After authorizing, the story will be available in `movieCompanyapp`.

See also

▶ The *Spring Security with Spring Social to access Facebook* recipe

▶ The *Spring Security with Spring Social to access Twitter* recipe

▶ The *Spring Security with multiple authentication providers* recipe

10
Spring Security with Spring Web Services

In this chapter we will cover:

- ▶ Applying Spring Security on RESTful web services
- ▶ Spring Security for Spring RESTful web service using the cURL tool
- ▶ Integrating Spring Security with Apache CXF RESTful service
- ▶ Integrating Spring Security with Apache CXF SOAP based web service
- ▶ Integrating Spring Security with Apache Camel

Introduction

SOAP (**Simple Object Access Protocol**) is an XML-based web service. It is used to transfer the request and response messages between web services.

REST (**Representational State Transfer**) is a means of sending data as XML, text, or JSON files over the HTTP protocol.

In this section we will apply Spring Security to web services. The normal flow of any web service is that the service WSDL or URL will be exposed to the end user. On application of Spring Security, the end users can be authenticated and authorized to use the services.

Applying Spring Security on RESTful web services

REST has become another means of providing web services.

The data can be shared across applications using XML, text, or in JSON format. REST web services are considered as lightweight web services.

Let's apply Spring Security for accessing the REST web service, so that only authorized users can access the RESTful web service. Since the RESTful web service is accessed with a URL and uses HTTP protocol we can easily apply the URL level security. This example demonstrates form-based authentication. But the user can also use BASIC and Digest Authentication.

The following are the annotations used with Spring to generate RESTful web services:

- `@PathVariable`
- `@RequestMapping`
- `@RequestMethod`

Getting ready

- Create a RESTful web service using Spring web service API
- Add Spring Security dependencies
- Add Spring filter configuration to the `Web.xml` file
- Configure the `application-security.xml` file
- Create an `AccessController` class to handle the login and logout actions
- Configure Spring Security in the application to authenticate the users

How to do it...

The following are the steps for integrating RESTful web services with Spring Security:

1. Let's create a `BookController` class with `@PathVariable`, as shown in the following code snippet:

```
package org.springframework.rest;
@Controller
public class BookController {
  private static final Map<Integer, Books> books = new
    HashMap<Integer, Books>();
  static {
    try {
```

```
      books.put(1, new Books(1, "Someone Like You",
        "Penguin", "Durjoy Datta-Nikita Singh"));
      books.put(2, new Books(2, "The Secret Wish List",
        "Westland", " Preeti Shenoy"));
      books.put(3, new Books(3, "Love Stories That Touched
        My Heart ", "Metro Reads", " Preeti Shenoy"));
    } catch (Exception e) {
      e.printStackTrace();
    }
  }
  @RequestMapping(value = "/books/{book_id}", method =
    RequestMethod.GET)
  @ResponseBody
  public Books findCharacter(@PathVariable int book_id) {
    return books.get(book_id);
  }
}
```

2. Create a `Books` POJO class with the `@JsonAutoDetect` annotation, as shown in the following code snippet:

```
@JsonAutoDetect
public class Books {
    private int book_id;
    private String book_name;
    private String book_publication;
    private String book_author;
    public Books(int book_id, String book_name, String
      book_publication, String book_author) {
      this.book_id = book_id;
      this.book_name = book_name;
      this.book_publication = book_publication;
      this.book_author = book_author;
    }
    public String getBook_author() {
      return book_author;
    }
    public void setBook_author(String book_author) {
      this.book_author = book_author;
    }
    public int getBook_id() {
      return book_id;
    }
    public void setBook_id(int book_id) {
      this.book_id = book_id;
    }
```

```
       public String getBook_name() {
         return book_name;
       }
       public void setBook_name(String book_name) {
         this.book_name = book_name;
       }
       public String getBook_publication() {
         return book_publication;
       }
       public void setBook_publication
         (String book_publication) {
         this.book_publication = book_publication;
       }
     }
```

3. Create an `AccessController` class to handle login and logout actions:

```
package org.springframework.booksservice;
@Controller
public class AccessController {
  @RequestMapping(value = "/", method =
    RequestMethod.GET)
  public String defaultPage(ModelMap map) {
    return "redirect:/login";
  }
  @RequestMapping(value = "/login", method =
    RequestMethod.GET)
  public String login(ModelMap model) {
    return "login";
  }
  @RequestMapping(value = "/accessdenied", method =
    RequestMethod.GET)
  public String loginerror(ModelMap model) {
    model.addAttribute("error", "true");
    return "denied";
  }
  @RequestMapping(value = "/logout", method =
    RequestMethod.GET)
  public String logout(ModelMap model) {
    return "logout";
  }
}
```

4. Configure the `Application-security.xml` file, as shown in the following code snippet:

```xml
<http auto-config="false"  use-expressions="true">
  <intercept-url pattern="/login" access="permitAll" />
  <intercept-url pattern="/logout" access="permitAll" />
  <intercept-url pattern="/accessdenied"
    access="permitAll" />
  <intercept-url pattern="/**"
    access="hasRole('ROLE_EDITOR')" />
  <form-login login-page="/login" default-target-
    url="/books" authentication-
    failure-url="/accessdenied" />
  <logout logout-success-url="/logout" />
</http>
<authentication-manager>
  <authentication-provider>
  <user-service>
    <user name="anjana" password="packt123"
      authorities="ROLE_EDITOR" />
  </user-service>
  </authentication-provider>
</authentication-manager>
```

How it works...

Access the URL: `http://localhost:8080/booksservice/books/1`. This is the REST-based URL, which is restricted from access using Spring Security. When the user calls the REST-based web service URL, Spring Security redirects the user to the login page. On successful authentication, the user is redirected to the authorized REST-based web service page.

The following is the workflow of the REST-based application with Spring Security. You will be redirected to the login page, as shown in the following screenshot:

On authentication and authorization, you will be able to access the RESTful web service, as shown in the following screenshot:

See also

- The *Integrating Spring Security with Apache CXF RESTful web service* recipe
- The *Integrating Spring Security with Apache CXF SOAP based web service* recipe
- The *Integrating Spring Security with Apache Camel* recipe

Spring Security for Spring RESTful web service using the cURL tool

In this example we are using the Spring Security API classes and interfaces explicitly. We will authenticate the RESTful web service using the `curl` command. With the cURL tool, you can transfer data with the URL. It can be used to test the authentication. It's the same book service example which has some explicit Spring Security related API classes such as `AuthenticationEntryPoint` and `SimpleURLAuthenticationSuccessHandler`. Here, the goal is to demonstrate their internal usage in Spring Security.

Getting ready

- Implement the `AuthenticationEntryPoint` interface and configure in the XML file
- Extend `SimpleUrlAuthenticationSuccessHandler` and configure in the XML file
- Configure the `Application-security.xml` file
- Add security related filters to the `Web.xml` file
- Download the cURL tool for your operating system

How to do it...

The following are the steps for applying the Spring Security authentication and authorization mechanism by using `AuthenticationEntryPoint` interface and `SimpleURLAuthenticationSuccessHandler` class:

1. The `AuthenticationEntryPoint` class is an entry class for authentication and it implements the `AuthenticationEntryPointImpl` class.

   ```java
   public final class AuthenticationEntryPointImpl implements
     AuthenticationEntryPoint {
     @Override
     public void commence(final HttpServletRequest request,
       final HttpServletResponse response, final
         AuthenticationException authException) throws
           IOException {
       response.sendError(HttpServletResponse.SC_UNAUTHORIZED,
         "Unauthorized");
     }
   }
   ```

2. Extend the `SimpleURLAuthenticationSuccessHandler` class, as shown in the following code snippet:

   ```java
   public class MySimpleUrlAuthenticationSuccessHandler
       extends SimpleUrlAuthenticationSuccessHandler {
     private RequestCache requestCache = new
       HttpSessionRequestCache();
     @Override
     public void onAuthenticationSuccess(final
       HttpServletRequest request, final HttpServletResponse
       response, final Authentication authentication) throws
       ServletException, IOException {
       final SavedRequest savedRequest =
         requestCache.getRequest(request, response);
       if (savedRequest == null) {
         clearAuthenticationAttributes(request);
         return;
       }
       final String targetUrlParameter =
         getTargetUrlParameter();
       if (isAlwaysUseDefaultTargetUrl() ||
         (targetUrlParameter != null &&
         StringUtils.hasText(request.getParameter
         (targetUrlParameter)))) {
         requestCache.removeRequest(request, response);
         clearAuthenticationAttributes(request);
   ```

```
        return;
      }
      clearAuthenticationAttributes(request);
    }
    public void setRequestCache(final RequestCache
      requestCache) {
      this.requestCache = requestCache;
    }
  }
```

3. Configure the `Application-security.xml` file.

```xml
<http entry-point-ref="authenticationEntryPoint">
  <intercept-url pattern="/**" access="ROLE_EDITOR"/>
  <form-login authentication-success-handler-
ref="mySuccessHandler" />
  <logout />
</http>
<beans:bean id="mySuccessHandler"
  class="org.springframework.booksservice.
    MySimpleUrlAuthenticationSuccessHandler"/>
<beans:bean id="authenticationEntryPoint"
  class="org.springframework.booksservice.
AuthenticationEntryPointImpl"/>
<authentication-manager>
  <authentication-provider>
    <user-service>
      <user name="anjana" password="packt123" authorities="ROLE_
EDITOR" />
    </user-service>
  </authentication-provider>
</authentication-manager>
</beans:beans>
```

How it works...

Now access the URL: `http://localhost:8080/booksservice/books/1`

You will see a page which says that you are not authorized to view the pages.

Let's use the cURL tool which gives us a cookie. The `200 OK` message implies that we are authenticated.

Command: `curl -i -X POST -d j_username=anjana -d j_password=packt123 http://localhost:8080/booksservice/j_spring_security_check`

`curl -i --header "Accept:application/json" -X GET -b cookies.txt http://localhost:8080/booksservice/books/1`

The cookies are stored in a file named `mycookies.txt`.

```
C:\WINDOWS\system32\cmd.exe                                        _ □ ×
operable program or batch file.                                        ▲

E:\curl-7.32.0-ssl-sspi-zlib-static-bin-w32>curl -i -X POST -d j_username=anjana
 -d j_password=packt123 http://localhost:8080/booksservice/j_spring_security_che
ck
HTTP/1.1 200 OK
Server: Apache-Coyote/1.1
Set-Cookie: JSESSIONID=FE6DCCDFE247F585840DA9E72D201FCD; Path=/booksservice
Content-Length: 0
Date: Tue, 10 Sep 2013 12:00:24 GMT
```

```
C:\WINDOWS\system32\cmd.exe                                        _ □ ×
operable program or batch file.                                        ▲

E:\curl-7.32.0-ssl-sspi-zlib-static-bin-w32>curl -i -X POST -d j_username=anjana
 -d j_password=packt123 http://localhost:8080/booksservice/j_spring_security_che
ck
HTTP/1.1 200 OK
Server: Apache-Coyote/1.1
Set-Cookie: JSESSIONID=FE6DCCDFE247F585840DA9E72D201FCD; Path=/booksservice
Content-Length: 0
Date: Tue, 10 Sep 2013 12:00:24 GMT

E:\curl-7.32.0-ssl-sspi-zlib-static-bin-w32>curl -i --header "Accept:application
/json" -X GET -b cookies.txt http://localhost:8080/booksservice/books/1
HTTP/1.1 200 OK
Server: Apache-Coyote/1.1
Content-Type: application/json;charset=UTF-8
Transfer-Encoding: chunked
Date: Tue, 10 Sep 2013 12:25:30 GMT

{"book_author":"Durjoy Datta-Nikita Singh","book_id":1,"book_name":"Someone Like
 You","book_publication":"Penguin"}
E:\curl-7.32.0-ssl-sspi-zlib-static-bin-w32>_
```

See also

▶ The *Integrating Spring Security with Apache CXF RESTful web service* recipe

▶ The *Integrating Spring Security with Apache CXF SOAP based web service* recipe

▶ The *Integrating Spring Security with Apache Camel* recipe

Integrating Spring Security with Apache CXF RESTful web service

In this section let us create an Apache CXF RESTful web service. It is an open source web service framework. Let's use BASIC authentication for this demonstration.

CXF supports contract-first and contract-last web services. It also supports RESTful web services.

Let us integrate Spring Security with CXF and authorize a RESTful web service.

Getting ready

- ▸ Add the cxf dependency to the pom file
- ▸ Set up the RESTful web service with CXF
- ▸ Configure the spring-security.xml file

How to do it...

The following are the steps to integrate Spring Security with Apache CXF RESTful web services:

1. Configure the Book POJO class.

```
@XmlRootElement(name = "book")
public class Book {
    private int book_id;
    private String book_name;
    private String book_publication;
    private String book_author;
    public Book(int book_id, String book_name, String
      book_publication, String book_author) {
      this.book_id = book_id;
      this.book_name = book_name;
      this.book_publication = book_publication;
      this.book_author = book_author;
    }
    public String getBook_author() {
      return book_author;
    }
    public void setBook_author(String book_author) {
      this.book_author = book_author;
    }
    public int getBook_id() {
      return book_id;
    }
    public void setBook_id(int book_id) {
      this.book_id = book_id;
    }
    public String getBook_name() {
      return book_name;
    }
    public void setBook_name(String book_name) {
      this.book_name = book_name;
    }
```

```
      public String getBook_publication() {
        return book_publication;
      }
      public void setBook_publication(String
        book_publication) {
        this.book_publication = book_publication;
      }
  }
```

2. Configure the `BookCollection` POJO class.

```
    @XmlType(name = "BookCollection")
    @XmlRootElement
    public class BookCollection {
      private Collection books;
      public BookCollection() {
      }
      public BookCollection(Collection books) {
        this.books = books;
      }
      @XmlElement(name="books")
      @XmlElementWrapper(name="books")
      public Collection getUsers() {
        return books;
      }

    }
```

3. Configure the `BookService` interface.

```
    public interface BookService {
        BookCollection getBooks();
        Book getBook(Integer id);
        Response add(Book book);
    }
```

4. Configure the `BookServiceImpl` class.

```
    @Path ("/services/")
    public class BookServiceImpl implements BookService {
      private static final Map<Integer, Book> books = new
        HashMap<Integer, Book>();
      private static int index = 4;
      static {
        try {
          books.put(1, new Book(1, "Someone Like You",
          "Penguin", "Durjoy Datta-Nikita Singh"));
```

```
                  books.put(2, new Book(2, "The Secret Wish List",
                  "Westland", " Preeti Shenoy"));
                  books.put(3, new Book(3, "Love Stories That
                  Touched My Heart ", "Metro Reads", " Preeti
                  Shenoy"));
              } catch (Exception e) {
                  e.printStackTrace();
              }
      }
      @Override
      @POST
      @Path("/book")
      @Consumes("application/json")
      public Response add(Book book) {
          System.out.println("Adding :" + book.getBook_name());
          book.setBook_id(index++);
          return Response.status(Response.Status.OK).build();
      }
      @Override
      @GET
      @Path("/book/{book_id}")
      @Produces("application/json")
      public Book getBook(@PathParam("book_id") Integer
        book_id) {
          return books.get(book_id);
      }
      @Override
      @GET
      @Path("/books")
      @Produces("application/json")
      public BookCollection getBooks() {
          return new BookCollection(books.values());
      }
  }
```

5. Configuring the `application-security.xml` file:

```
<sec:global-method-security pre-post-
  annotations="enabled" />
<sec:http auto-config="true"  use-expressions="true">
  <sec:intercept-url pattern="/**"
    access="hasRole('ROLE_EDITOR')"/>
  <sec:http-basic></sec:http-basic>
  <sec:logout logout-success-url="/logout" />
</sec:http>
```

```xml
<import resource="classpath:META-INF/cxf/cxf.xml" />
<import resource="classpath:META-INF/cxf/cxf-
  servlet.xml"/>
<jaxrs:server address="/" id="myService">
  <jaxrs:serviceBeans>
    <ref bean="bookserviceImpl"/>
  </jaxrs:serviceBeans>
  <jaxrs:providers>
    <ref bean="jacksonProvider"/>
  </jaxrs:providers>
</jaxrs:server>
<bean id="jacksonProvider"
class="org.codehaus.jackson.jaxrs.
  JacksonJaxbJsonProvider"/>
<bean id="bookserviceImpl"
class="org.springframework.booksservice.
  BookServiceImpl"/>
<sec:authentication-manager>
  <sec:authentication-provider>
    <sec:user-service>
      <sec:user name="anjana" password="packt123"
        authorities="ROLE_EDITOR" />
    </sec:user-service>
  </sec:authentication-provider>
</sec:authentication-manager>
</beans>
```

6. Configure the `Web.xml` file.

```xml
<!-- The definition of the Root Spring Container shared
  by all Servlets and Filters -->
<context-param>
  <param-name>contextConfigLocation</param-name>
  <param-value>/WEB-INF/spring/application-
    security.xml</param-value>
</context-param>
<!-- Creates the Spring Container shared by all Servlets
  and Filters -->
<listener>
<listener-class>org.springframework.web.context.
  ContextLoaderListener</listener-class>
</listener>
<!-- Processes application requests -->
<servlet>
  <servlet-name>cxf</servlet-name>
```

```
    <servlet-class>org.apache.cxf.transport.
      servlet.CXFServlet</servlet-class>
    <load-on-startup>1</load-on-startup>
  </servlet>
  <servlet-mapping>
    <servlet-name>cxf</servlet-name>
    <url-pattern>/services/*</url-pattern>
  </servlet-mapping>
  <!-- Spring child -->
  <!-- <servlet>
  <servlet-name>bookservice_cxf</servlet-name>
    <servlet-class>org.springframework.web.servlet.
      DispatcherServlet</servlet-class>
    <load-on-startup>1</load-on-startup>
  </servlet>
  <servlet-mapping>
    <servlet-name>bookservice_cxf</servlet-name>
    <url-pattern>/bookservice_cxf/*</url-pattern>
  </servlet-mapping>-->
  <filter>
    <filter-name>springSecurityFilterChain</filter-name>
    <filter-class>org.springframework.web.filter.
      DelegatingFilterProxy</filter-class>
  </filter>
  <filter-mapping>
    <filter-name>springSecurityFilterChain</filter-name>
    <url-pattern>/*</url-pattern>
  </filter-mapping>
</web-app>
```

How it works...

The RESTful service is provided by the CXF framework in this example. Then the application is integrated with Spring Security in order to provide secured authentication and authorization module to RESTful web service. Spring Security filter chain manages the authentication and authorization process. When you access the service, you will be prompted to log in, as shown in the following screenshot. After login, you can view the RESTful data. The Mozilla Firefox browser will prompt the user to download the data in a file format.

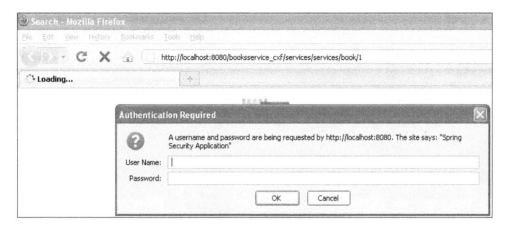

Now access the URL: `http://localhost:8080/booksservice_cxf/services/services/book/1`

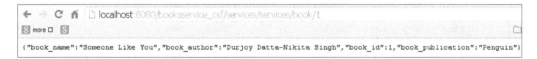

See also

▸ The *Integrating Spring Security with Apache CXF RESTful web service* recipe

▸ The *Integrating Spring Security with Apache Camel* recipe

Integrating Spring Security with Apache CXF SOAP based web service

In this section, let's create a SOAP-based web service. We will demonstrate the integration of Spring Security with Apache CXF SOAP-based web service.

Creation of SOAP-based web service has become a simple process with Apache CXF.

Getting ready

▸ Add the CXF-SOAP dependency to the `pom` file.

▸ Add Spring Security-based dependency to the `pom` file.

▸ Set up a SOAP-based web service with `interface` and an `Impl` class.

▸ Configure the `spring-security.xml` file.

▶ Add jars to the `Tomcat_7.0/lib` folder as a part of setup. Tomcat requires the following jar files in its `lib` folder to work with CXF web services. Absence of these jars can cause some errors:

❑ `streambuffer.jar`

❑ `stax-ex`

❑ `jaxws-ap-2.1`

❑ `jaxws-rt`

How to do it...

The following are the steps to integrate Apache CXF SOAP-based web service with Spring Security:

1. The `Book` POJO has getter and setter methods. It also has a parameterized constructor. The `Book` POJO is used in the `BookService` interface, to give details on `Book` that is requested from the client application.

```
package org.packt.cxf.domain;
public class Book {
  private int book_id;
  private String book_name;
  private String book_publication;
  private String book_author;
  public Book() {
  }
  public Book(int book_id, String book_name, String
    book_publication, String book_author) {
    this.book_id = book_id;
    this.book_name = book_name;
    this.book_publication = book_publication;
    this.book_author = book_author;
  }
  public String getBook_author() {
    return book_author;
    }
    public void setBook_author(String book_author) {
        this.book_author = book_author;
  }
  public int getBook_id() {
    return book_id;
  }
  public void setBook_id(int book_id) {
```

```
    this.book_id = book_id;
  }
  public String getBook_name() {
    return book_name;
  }
  public void setBook_name(String book_name) {
    this.book_name = book_name;
  }
  public String getBook_publication() {
    return book_publication;
  }
  public void setBook_publication(String book_publication)
    {
    this.book_publication = book_publication;
  }
}
```

2. The `BookService` interface is created with the `@WebService` annotation, in which `getBookDetails` is the service method in the WSDL.

```
package org.packt.cxf.service;
import javax.jws.WebService;
import org.packt.cxf.domain.Book;
@WebService
public interface BookService {
  public Book getBookDetails(int book_id);
}
```

3. The `BookServiceImpl` class is the implementation class of the `BookService` interface, and it is configured as an end point interface using `@webservice` annotation package `org.packt.cxf.service`.

```
import java.util.HashMap;
import java.util.Map;
import javax.jws.WebService;
import org.packt.cxf.domain.Book;
@WebService(endpointInterface =
  "org.packt.cxf.service.BookService")
public class BookServiceImpl implements BookService{
    private static final Map<Integer, Book> books = new
      HashMap<Integer, Book>();
    private static int index = 4;
    static {
      try {
        books.put(1, new Book(1, "Someone Like You",
          "Penguin", "Durjoy Datta-Nikita Singh"));
```

```
        books.put(2, new Book(2, "The Secret Wish List",
          "Westland", " Preeti Shenoy"));
        books.put(3, new Book(3, "Love Stories That Touched
          My Heart ", "Metro Reads", " Preeti Shenoy"));
      } catch (Exception e) {
        e.printStackTrace();
      }
    }
    @Override
    public Book getBookDetails(int book_id) {
      return books.get(book_id);
    }}
```

4. In the `Cxf-servlet.xml` file, we register the web service interface and the implementation class.

```
<beans xmlns="http://www.springframework.org/schema/beans"
xmlns:xsi="http://www.w3.org/2001/XMLSchema-instance"
  xmlns:jaxws="http://cxf.apache.org/jaxws"
xsi:schemaLocation="
  http://www.springframework.org/schema/beans
  http://www.springframework.org/schema/beans/spring-
    beans.xsd
  http://cxf.apache.org/jaxws
  http://cxf.apache.org/schemas/jaxws.xsd">
<import resource="classpath:META-INF/cxf/cxf.xml" />
<import resource="classpath:META-INF/cxf/cxf-servlet.xml"
  />
<import resource="classpath:META-INF/cxf/cxf-extension-
  http.xml" />
<import resource="classpath:META-INF/cxf/cxf-extension-
  soap.xml" />
<jaxws:endpoint id="bookService"implementor="org.
  packt.cxf.service.BookServiceImpl"
  address="/BookService" />
</beans>
```

5. In the `Web.xml` file, we give reference to the location of `cxf-servlet.xml` and configure `CXFSservlet`.

```
<web-app version="2.5"
  xmlns="http://java.sun.com/xml/ns/javaee"
  xmlns:xsi="http://www.w3.org/2001/XMLSchema-instance"
  xsi:schemaLocation="http://java.sun.com/xml/ns/javaee
  http://java.sun.com/xml/ns/javaee/web-app_2_5.xsd">
  <display-name>SampleWSCxf</display-name>
  <listener>
```

```
      <listener-class>org.springframework.web.context.
        ContextLoaderListener</listener-class>
    </listener>
    <context-param>
      <param-name>contextConfigLocation</param-name>
      <param-value>WEB-INF/cxf-servlet.xml</param-value>
    </context-param>
    <servlet>
      <servlet-name>CXFServlet</servlet-name>
      <servlet-class>org.apache.cxf.transport.servlet.
        CXFServlet</servlet-class>
      <load-on-startup>1</load-on-startup>
    </servlet>
    <servlet-mapping>
      <servlet-name>CXFServlet</servlet-name>
      <url-pattern>/*</url-pattern>
    </servlet-mapping>
  </web-app>
```

How it works...

In this section we demonstrate basic authentication on web service. Access the URL:
`http://localhost:8080/bookservice/`

We have used the CXF framework to create a SOAP-based web service. When the URL is accessed by the user, the expected behavior is to give access to the WSDL and its services. But the Spring Security interrupts the request and pops up a login dialog box for the user. On successful authentication, the user gets to access the WSDL.

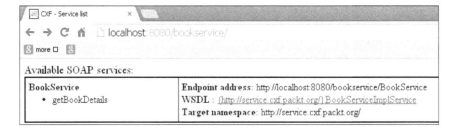

Generated WSDL is available at the following URL: `http://localhost:8080/bookservice/BookService?wsdl`

```
<wsdl:definitions
  xmlns:ns1="http://cxf.apache.org/bindings/xformat"
  xmlns:soap="http://schemas.xmlsoap.org/wsdl/soap/"
  xmlns:tns="http://service.cxf.packt.org/"
  xmlns:wsdl="http://schemas.xmlsoap.org/wsdl/"
  xmlns:xsd="http://www.w3.org/2001/XMLSchema"
  name="BookServiceImplService"
  targetNamespace="http://service.cxf.packt.org/">
  <wsdl:types>
  <xs:schema xmlns:tns="http://service.cxf.packt.org/"
    xmlns:xs="http://www.w3.org/2001/XMLSchema"
    elementFormDefault="unqualified"
    targetNamespace="http://service.cxf.packt.org/"
    version="1.0">
  <xs:element name="getBookDetails"
    type="tns:getBookDetails"/>
  <xs:element name="getBookDetailsResponse"
    type="tns:getBookDetailsResponse"/>
  <xs:complexType name="getBookDetails">
    <xs:sequence>
      <xs:element name="arg0" type="xs:int"/>
    </xs:sequence>
  </xs:complexType>
  <xs:complexType name="getBookDetailsResponse">
    <xs:sequence>
      <xs:element minOccurs="0" name="return"
        type="tns:book"/>
    </xs:sequence>
  </xs:complexType>
  <xs:complexType name="book">
    <xs:sequence>
      <xs:element minOccurs="0" name="book_author"
        type="xs:string"/>
      <xs:element name="book_id" type="xs:int"/>
```

```
      <xs:element minOccurs="0" name="book_name"
        type="xs:string"/>
      <xs:element minOccurs="0" name="book_publication"
        type="xs:string"/>
      </xs:sequence>
    </xs:complexType>
  </xs:schema>
</wsdl:types>
<wsdl:message name="getBookDetails">
  <wsdl:part element="tns:getBookDetails"
    name="parameters"></wsdl:part>
</wsdl:message>
<wsdl:message name="getBookDetailsResponse">
  <wsdl:part element="tns:getBookDetailsResponse"
    name="parameters"></wsdl:part>
  </wsdl:message>
<wsdl:portType name="BookService">
  <wsdl:operation name="getBookDetails">
    <wsdl:input message="tns:getBookDetails"
      name="getBookDetails"></wsdl:input>
    <wsdl:outputmessage="tns:getBookDetailsResponse"
      name="getBookDetailsResponse"></wsdl:output>
  </wsdl:operation>
</wsdl:portType>
<wsdl:bindingname="BookServiceImplServiceSoapBinding"
  type="tns:BookService">
  <soap:bindingstyle="document"
   transport="http://schemas.xmlsoap.org/soap/http"/>
    <wsdl:operationname="getBookDetails">
      <soap:operationsoapAction=""style="document"/>
    <wsdl:inputname="getBookDetails">
      <soap:bodyuse="literal"/>
    </wsdl:input>
    <wsdl:outputname="getBookDetailsResponse">
      <soap:bodyuse="literal"/>
    </wsdl:output>
  </wsdl:operation>
</wsdl:binding>
<wsdl:servicename="BookServiceImplService">
  <wsdl:portbinding="tns:BookServiceImplServiceSoap
    Binding"name="BookServiceImplPort">
    <soap:addresslocation="http://localhost:8080
      /bookservice/BookService"/>
  </wsdl:port>
</wsdl:service>
</wsdl:definitions>
```

- The *Integrating Spring Security with Apache CXF RESTful web service* recipe
- The *Integrating Spring Security with Apache Camel* recipe

Integrating Spring Security with Apache Camel

Apache Camel can be used to define rules for routing and mediating applications. Spring Security can be used with Apache Camel to authenticate the router. Spring Security authentication policy object controls the access to the router. The Spring Security authentication policy object contains the role information and has reference to the Spring authentication manager. You can download the source code from the website.

Getting ready

- Create Camel context
- Add routing rules using the XML configurations
- In Spring XML file configure the following:
    - Access decision manager
    - Role voter
    - Authentication manager
    - User details service
- Configure the authentication policy object with authorities
- Add the `camel-spring-security` dependency

How to do it...

The following are the steps to integrate Apache Camel with Spring Security:

1. Create the `Camel-context.xml` file and also define the routing rules with Spring Security.

    ```
    <spring-security:http realm="User Access Realm">
      <spring-security:intercept-url
        pattern="/apachecamel/**"      access="ROLE_EDITOR"/>
      <spring-security:http-basic/>
      <spring-security:remember-me/>
    </spring-security:http>
    ```

```xml
<spring-security:authentication-manager
  alias="authenticationManager">
  <spring-security:authentication-provider user-service-
    ref="userDetailsService"/>
</spring-security:authentication-manager>
<spring-security:user-service id="userDetailsService">
  <spring-security:user name="anju" password="anju123"
    authorities="ROLE_EDITOR,ROLE_AUTHOR"/>
  <spring-security:user name="shami" password="shami123"
    authorities="ROLE_EDITOR"/>
</spring-security:user-service>
<bean id="accessDecisionManager"
  class="org.springframework.security.access.
    vote.AffirmativeBased">
  <property name="allowIfAllAbstainDecisions"
    value="true"/>
  <property name="decisionVoters">
    <list>
      <bean class="org.springframework.security
        .access.vote.RoleVoter"/>
    </list>
  </property>
</bean>
<!-- The Policy for checking the authentication role of
  AUTHOR -->
<authorizationPolicy id="author" access="ROLE_AUTHOR"
  authenticationManager="authenticationManager"
  accessDecisionManager="accessDecisionManager"
  xmlns="http://camel.apache.org/schema/spring-
    security"/>
<!-- The Policy for checking the authentication role of
  EDITOR -->
<authorizationPolicy id="editor" access="ROLE_EDITOR"
  xmlns="http://camel.apache.org/schema/spring-
    security"/>
<camelContext id="myCamelContext"
  xmlns="http://camel.apache.org/schema/spring">
  <!-- Catch the authorization exception and set the
    Access Denied message back -->
  <onException>
  <exception>org.apache.camel.
    CamelAuthorizationException</exception>
  <handled>
    <constant>true</constant>
  </handled>
  <transform>
```

```
            <simple>Access Denied with the Policy of
              ${exception.policyId} !</simple>
            </transform>
          </onException>
          <route>
            <from uri="servlet:///editor"/>
            <!-- wrap the route in the policy which enforces
              security check -->
            <policy ref="editor">
              <transform>
                <simple>Normal user can access this
                  service</simple>
              </transform>
            </policy>
          </route>
          <route>
            <from uri="servlet:///author"/>
            <!-- wrap the route in the policy which enforces
              security check -->
            <policy ref="author">
              <transform>
                <simple>Call the admin operation OK</simple>
              </transform>
            </policy>
          </route>
        </camelContext>
      </beans>
```

2. Configure Camel servlet in `Web.xml`.

```
    <!-- location of spring xml files -->
    <context-param>
      <param-name>contextConfigLocation</param-name>
      <param-value>classpath:camel-context.xml</param-value>
    </context-param>
    <!-- the listener that kick-starts Spring -->
    <listener>
      <listener-class>org.springframework.web.
        context.ContextLoaderListener</listener-class>
    </listener>
    <filter>
      <filter-name>springSecurityFilterChain</filter-name>
      <filter-class>org.springframework.web.
        filter.DelegatingFilterProxy</filter-class>
    </filter>
```

```xml
<filter-mapping>
  <filter-name>springSecurityFilterChain</filter-name>
  <url-pattern>/*</url-pattern>
</filter-mapping>
<servlet>
  <servlet-name>CamelServlet</servlet-name>
  <servlet-class>org.apache.camel.component.
    servlet.CamelHttpTransportServlet</servlet-class>
  <load-on-startup>1</load-on-startup>
</servlet>
<servlet-mapping>
  <servlet-name>CamelServlet</servlet-name>
  <url-pattern>/apachecamel/*</url-pattern>
</servlet-mapping>
</web-app>
```

How it works...

Now access the URL: `http://localhost:8080/apachecamel/editor`

The `camel-context.xml` file has routing rules; the location of the `camel-context.xml` file is configured in `Web.xml` along with `CamelServlet` to handle the routing mechanism. The `<authorizationpolicy>` tag handles the authentication and authorization of the resources configured in the `spring-security.xml` file. The `<spring-security:user-service>` tag has details of the users and roles to whom the access can be given before routing the requests. The following is the workflow of Apache Camel interrupting the routing process using Spring Security. The user is authorized on either of the two roles: EDITOR or AUTHOR.

See also

▶ The *Integrating Spring Security with Apache CXF RESTful web service* recipe

▶ The *Integrating Spring Security with Apache Camel* recipe

11
More on Spring Security

In this chapter we will cover:

- ▸ Spring Security with multiple authentication providers
- ▸ Spring Security with multiple input authentications
- ▸ Spring Security with Captcha integration
- ▸ Spring Security with JAAS

Introduction

In this chapter we will see some more examples of Spring Security. Let's see how we can integrate Spring Security with multiple authentication providers. We will also see an example of authentication using Spring with multiple inputs.

Spring Security with multiple authentication providers

Spring Security provides an option to add many authentication providers. The filter chain checks with each and every authentication provider until it gets authenticated successfully.

In this section, let's see how to configure multiple authentication providers and how Spring does the authentication with multiple authentication providers.

For example, we are using the `horrormovie` application in which authentication and authorization is handled by Spring Security with database.

Getting ready

- ▸ Create a maven web project
- ▸ Add the `spring-security` dependency
- ▸ Add the spring-core related dependency
- ▸ Configure the Spring context listener in the `Web.xml` file
- ▸ Create the `AddHorroMovieController.java` controller and add the request mapping methods for addition, deletion, and listing
- ▸ Edit the `application-security.xml` file with another authentication provider

How to do it...

The following are the steps to integrate multiple authentication providers with Spring Security:

1. Edit the `application-security.xml` file.

```
<authentication-manager alias="authentication Manager">
  <authentication-provider>
    <jdbc-user-service data-source-ref="tenant1DataSource"
      users-by-username-query=" select username, password
      ,'true' as enabled from users where username=?"
      authorities-by-username-query=" select u.username
      as username, ur.authority as authority from users
      u, user_roles ur where u.user_id = ur.user_id and
      u.username =?" />
  </authentication-provider>
  <authentication-provider>
    <user-service>
    <user name="anjana" password="anjana123"
      authorities="ROLE_EDITOR"/>
    <user name="raghu" password="raghu123"
      authorities="ROLE_AUTHOR"/>
    <user name="shami" password="shami123"
      authorities="ROLE_EDITOR"/>
    </user-service>
  </authentication-provider>
</authentication-manager>
```

How it works...

Deploy the application on a GlassFish application server; access the following URL: `http://localhost:8080/list` and log in with username/password (`Vikash/Vikash123`).

This is the user created in the derby database with access (`ROLE_EDITOR`).

Then log out and log in again with username as `shami` and password as `shami123`. Here the user is authenticated by both the authentication providers in a sequential manner.

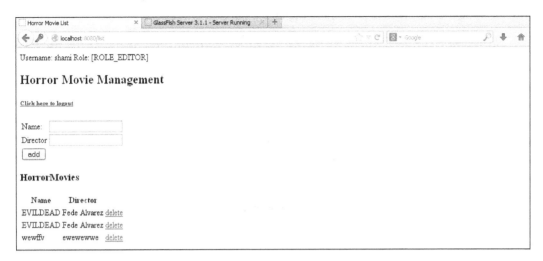

See also

▸ The *Spring Security with multiple input authentications* recipe

▸ The *Spring Security with Captcha integration* recipe

▸ The *Spring Security with JAAS* recipe

Spring Security with multiple input authentications

In this section, we will demonstrate multiple input authentications. This is also called two factor authentications. So far, in all our examples, we are authenticating against username and password. In this example, we will provide another field for phone number along with username. It is the same `horrormovie` application with hibernate and derby database.

Getting ready

▸ Create a custom filter to handle the new login form

▸ Configure the custom filter in your `Springsecurity.xml` file

▸ Update the `UserDetailsService` implementation class to handle the additional input

▸ Add an extra column named `MOBILE_NO` in your database

▸ Update the `login.jsp` file to take `MOBILE_NO` as input

How to do it...

The following are the steps to implement multiple input authentications with Spring Security:

1. Create a custom filter named `MultipleInputAuthenticationFilter` to extract the extra mobile number parameter.

```java
public class MultipleInputAuthenticationFilter extends
  UsernamePasswordAuthenticationFilter{
  private String extraParameter = "mobile_no";

  public String getExtraParameter() {
      return extraParameter;
  }

  public void setExtraParameter(String extraParameter) {
    this.extraParameter = extraParameter;
  }
  private String delimiter = ":";

  @Override
  protected String obtainUsername(HttpServletRequest
    request)
    {
      String username =
        request.getParameter(getUsernameParameter());
      String mobile_no =
        request.getParameter(getExtraParameter());
      String combinedUsername = username + getDelimiter()
        + mobile_no;
      System.out.println("Combined username = " +
        combinedUsername);
      return combinedUsername;
    }

  public String getDelimiter()
  {
    return this.delimiter;
  }
  /**
    * @param delimiter The delimiter string used to
      separate the username and extra input values in the
      * string returned by <code>obtainUsername()</code>
  */
  public void setDelimiter(String delimiter) {
    this.delimiter = delimiter;
  }
```

2. Update the `application-security.xml` file to handle the custom filter.

```xml
<global-method-security pre-post-annotations="enabled" />
  <http auto-config="false" use-expressions="true"
    entry-point-ref="loginUrlAuthenticationEntryPoint">
    <intercept-url pattern="/login" access="permitAll" />
    <intercept-url pattern="/logout" access="permitAll"
      />
    <intercept-url pattern="/accessdenied"
      access="permitAll" />
    <intercept-url pattern="/list"
      access="hasRole('ROLE_EDITOR')" />
    <intercept-url pattern="/add"
      access="hasRole('ROLE_EDITOR')" />
    <custom-filter position="FORM_LOGIN_FILTER"
      ref="multipleInputAuthenticationFilter" />
    <!--<form-login login-page="/login" default-target-
      url="/list" authentication-failure-
      url="/accessdenied" />-->
    <logout logout-success-url="/logout" />
  </http>
  <authentication-manager alias="authenticationManager">
    <authentication-provider user-service-
      ref="MyUserDetails">
      <password-encoder hash="plaintext" />
    </authentication-provider>
  </authentication-manager>
  <beans:bean id="multipleInputAuthenticationFilter"
    class="com.packt.springsecurity.controller.
      MultipleInputAuthenticationFilter">
    <beans:property name="authenticationManager"
      ref="authenticationManager" />
    <beans:property name="authenticationFailureHandler"
      ref="failureHandler" />
    <beans:property name="authenticationSuccessHandler"
      ref="successHandler" />
    <beans:property name="filterProcessesUrl"
      value="/j_spring_security_check" />
    <beans:property name="postOnly" value="true" />
    <beans:property name="extraParameter" value="mobile_no"
      />
  </beans:bean>
  <beans:bean id="horrorMovieDAO"
    class="com.packt.springsecurity.dao.
      HorrorMovieDaoImpl" />
  <beans:bean id="horrorMovieManager"
    class="com.packt.springsecurity.
```

```
                  service.HorrorMovieManagerImpl" />
        <beans:bean id="UsersDAO"
          class="com.packt.springsecurity.dao.UsersDAOImpl" />
        <beans:bean id="UsersManager"
        class="com.packt.springsecurity.
          service.UsersManagerImpl" />
        <beans:bean id="UserRoleDAO"
          class="com.packt.springsecurity.dao.
            UserRoleDAOImpl" />
        <beans:bean id="UserRoleManager"
          class="com.packt.springsecurity.
            service.UserRoleManagerImpl" />
        <beans:bean id="loginUrlAuthenticationEntryPoint"
          class="org.springframework.security.web.
            authentication.LoginUrlAuthenticationEntryPoint">
          <beans:property name="loginFormUrl" value="/login" />
        </beans:bean>
        <beans:bean id="successHandler"
          class="org.springframework.security.web.
          authentication.SavedRequestAwareAuthentication
          SuccessHandler">
          <beans:property name="defaultTargetUrl" value="/list"
            />
        </beans:bean>

        <beans:bean id="failureHandler"
          class="org.springframework.security.web.
          authentication.SimpleUrlAuthentication
          FailureHandler">
          <beans:property name="defaultFailureUrl"
            value="/accessdenied" />
        </beans:bean>
        <beans:bean id="MyUserDetails"
          class="com.packt.springsecurity.service.MyUserDetails" />
        </beans:beans>
```

3. Update `UsersDAOImpl` to handle the extra input.

```
@Override
    @Transactional
    public Users findByUserNameMobile(String userName, String
      mobile_no) {
      List<Users> userList = new ArrayList<Users>();
      Query query = (Query) sessionFactory.
      getCurrentSession().createQuery
      ("from Users u where u.userName = :userName and
      u.mobile_no=:mobile_no");
      query.setParameter("userName", userName);
```

```
      query.setInteger("mobile_no",
        Integer.parseInt(mobile_no));
      userList = query.list();
      if (userList.size() > 0) {
        return userList.get(0);
      } else {
        return null;
      }
    }
```

4. Implement the methods in the MyUserDetails class, which implements the UserDetailsService interface to handle the extra inputs.

```
public UserDetails loadUserByUsername(String str)
  throws UsernameNotFoundException {
  String[] splitstring = str.split(":");
  if (splitstring.length < 2) {
    System.out.println("User did not enter both
      username and mobile number.");
    throw new UsernameNotFoundException("Must specify both
      username and mobile number");
  }
  String username = splitstring[0];
  String mobile = splitstring[1];

  System.out.println("Username = " + username);
  System.out.println("Mobile = " + mobile);

  Users users = UsersDAO.findByUserNameMobile(username,
    mobile);
  boolean enabled = true;
  boolean accountNonExpired = true;
  boolean credentialsNonExpired = true;
  boolean accountNonLocked = true;
  return new User(
    users.getUserName(),
    users.getUserPassword(),
    enabled,
    accountNonExpired,
    credentialsNonExpired,
    accountNonLocked,
    getAuthorities(users.getRole().getRoleId().intValue()));
}
```

How it works...

Access the following URL: `http://localhost:8080/SpringSecurity_MultipleInputAuth/login`

The user is authenticated not just with the username and password as demonstrated in all the applications used in the book, but also with the mobile number parameter.

When the user submits the information in the login page and hits on **SubmitQuery**, the username and mobile number gets clubbed with a delimiter and Spring Security will invoke the `MyUserDetails` class, which will again split the parameter and authenticate the user based on the inputs provided by the user using hibernate.

On successful authentication, the user is redirected to the authorized page.

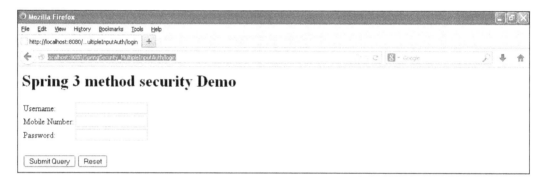

See also

- The *Spring Security with multiple authentication providers* recipe
- The *Spring Security with Captcha integration* recipe
- The *Spring Security with JAAS* recipe

Spring Security with Captcha integration

Let us demonstrate the integration of Spring Security with Captcha. We have downloaded a `Kaptcha.jar` Captcha provider for this purpose. We need to install the jar file into the maven local repository for the application to work.

The example is an extension of the previous recipe where an additional input, mobile number, was considered for authorization and authentication by Spring Security. In this example, we will get the code for username and password from the user along with the Captcha code. The username is authenticated against the database, and the requested Captcha and the Captcha entered by the user are also compared.

When the entire conditions match, the user is said to be authenticated or else the authentication is a failure.

Getting ready

- ▶ Add the `Kaptcha` servlet to the `Web.xml` file
- ▶ Configure the custom filter in your `Springsecurity.xml` file
- ▶ Update the `UserDetailsService` implementation class to handle `Kaptcha`
- ▶ Update the `login.jsp` file to take `Kaptcha` as an input
- ▶ Extend `UsernamePasswordAuthenticationFilter`

How to do it...

The following are the steps to integrate Spring Security with Captcha:

1. Add the `Kaptcha` servlet to the `Web.xml` file.

```
<servlet>
  <servlet-name>Kaptcha</servlet-name>
  <servlet-class>
    com.google.code.kaptcha.servlet.KaptchaServlet
  </servlet-class>
</servlet>
<servlet-mapping>
  <servlet-name>Kaptcha</servlet-name>
  <url-pattern>/kaptcha.jpg</url-pattern>
</servlet-mapping>
```

2. Update the `application-security.xml` to handle the custom filter.

```
<beans:bean id="multipleInputAuthenticationFilter"
  class="com.packt.springsecurity.controller.
    MultipleInputAuthenticationFilter">
  <beans:property name="authenticationManager"
    ref="authenticationManager" />
  <beans:property name="authenticationFailureHandler"
    ref="failureHandler" />
  <beans:property name="authenticationSuccessHandler"
    ref="successHandler" />
  <beans:property name="filterProcessesUrl"
    value="/j_spring_security_check" />
  <beans:property name="postOnly" value="true" />
  <beans:property name="extraParameter" value="kaptcha"
    />
</beans:bean>
```

3. Update `UsersDAOImpl` to handle the extra input.

```java
@Override
@Transactional
public Users findByUserNameCaptcha(String userName, String
  kaptchaReceived, String kaptchaExpected) {
    List<Users> userList = new ArrayList<Users>();
    Query query = (Query) sessionFactory.
      getCurrentSession().createQuery("from Users u where
        u.userName = :userName");
    query.setParameter("userName", userName);
    userList = query.list();
    if (userList.size()>0 &&
      kaptchaReceived.equalsIgnoreCase(kaptchaExpected)) {
        return (Users)userList.get(0);
    } else {
        return null;
    }
}
```

4. Update the `UserDetailsService` class to handle the extra input.

```java
public UserDetails loadUserByUsername(String str)
  throws UsernameNotFoundException {
  String[] splitstring = str.split(":");
  if (splitstring.length < 2) {
    System.out.println("User did not enter both username
      and captcha code.");
    throw new UsernameNotFoundException("Must specify
      both username captcha code");
  }
  String username = splitstring[0];
  String kaptchaReceived = splitstring[1];
  String kaptchaExpected = splitstring[2];
  Users users = UsersDAO.findByUserNameCaptcha(username,
    kaptchaReceived,kaptchaExpected);
  boolean enabled = true;
  boolean accountNonExpired = true;
  boolean credentialsNonExpired = true;
  boolean accountNonLocked = true;
  return new User(
    users.getUserName(),
    users.getUserPassword(),
    enabled,
    accountNonExpired,
```

```
        credentialsNonExpired,
        accountNonLocked,
        getAuthorities(users.getRole().
           getRoleId().intValue())
   );
}
```

5. Extend `UsernamePasswordAuthenticationFilter` and override
   the `obtainUsername (HttpServletRequest request)` method in the
   `MultipleInputAuthenticationFilter` class.

```
@Override
   protected String obtainUsername(HttpServletRequest
      request) {
   String username =
      request.getParameter(getUsernameParameter());
   String kaptcha =
      request.getParameter(getExtraParameter());
   String kaptchaExpected = (String)
      request.getSession().getAttribute
      (com.google.code.kaptcha.Constants.
      KAPTCHA_SESSION_KEY);
   String combinedUsername = username + getDelimiter() +
      kaptcha + getDelimiter() + kaptchaExpected;
   System.out.println("Combined username = " +
      combinedUsername);
   return combinedUsername;
   }
```

How it works...

Access the following URL:

`http://localhost:8080/SpringSecurity_MultipleInputAuth/login`

The `Kaptcha` servlet displays different diagrams for the user on the browser.

The value entered by the user and the value generated by `Kaptcha` are compared in the `UsersDAOImpl.java` class along with the `Username` field from the database. When entire conditions match, that is, `Kaptcha` entered by the user should be the same as `Kaptcha` displayed by the browser and the username should be present in the database, then the user is said to be authenticated. The user is redirected to the authenticated and authorized page.

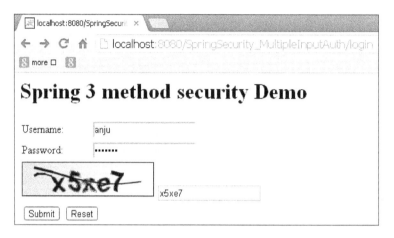

See also

▸ The *Spring Security with multiple authentication providers* recipe

▸ The *Spring Security with multiple input authentications* recipe

▸ The *Spring Security with JAAS* recipe

Spring Security with JAAS

In *Chapter 1, Basic Security*, we have already demonstrated how to use JAAS configuration in JBOSS for authentication and authorization. Spring Security also provides a full support to implement JAAS-based authentication. We need to configure `DefaultJaasAuthenticationProvider` as the authentication provider. In this section, we will demonstrate integration of Spring Security with JAAS.

Let us see some of the JAAS-based classes and interfaces offered by Spring Security APIs:

▸ `org.springframework.security.authentication.jaas`

▸ `AbstractJaasAuthenticationProvider`

▸ `AuthorityGranter`

- DefaultJaasAuthenticationProvider
- DefaultLoginExceptionResolver
- JaasAuthenticationCallbackHandler
- JaasAuthenticationToken
- JaasGrantedAuthority
- JaasNameCallbackHandler
- LoginExceptionResolver
- SecurityContextLoginModule

Getting ready

- Implement the `AuthorityGranter` interface by `org.springframework.security.authentication.jaas.AuthorityGranter`
- Implement the `LoginModule` interface by `javax.security.auth.spi.LoginModule`
- Configure the `DefaultJaasAuthenticationProvider` class in the `context.xml` file. Implement the `AuthorityGranter` interface and its configurations.

How to do it...

The following are the steps for implementing JAAS with Spring Security:

1. Implement the `AuthorityGranter` class using the `AuthorityGranterImpl` class.

```
public class AuthorityGranterImpl implements
  AuthorityGranter {
  public Set<String> grant(Principal principal) {
    if (principal.getName().equals("publisher"))
      return Collections.singleton("PUBLISHER");
    else
      return Collections.singleton("EDITOR");
  }
}
```

2. Implement the `LoginModule` class, which is available in the `javax.security.auth.spi` package, using the `LoginModuleImpl` class.

```
public class LoginModuleImpl implements LoginModule {
  private String password;
  private String username;
  private Subject subject;
```

```java
public boolean login() throws LoginException {
  // Check the password against the username "publisher"
    or "editor"
  if (username == null || (!username.equals("publisher")
    && !username.equals("editor"))) {
    throw new LoginException("User not valid");
  }
  if (password == null ||
    (!password.equals("publisher123") &&
      !password.equals("editor123"))) {
    throw new LoginException("Password not valid");
  } else {
    subject.getPrincipals().add(new
      UserPrincipal(username));
    return true;
  }
}

@Override
public boolean abort() throws LoginException {
  // TODO Auto-generated method stub
  return false;
}

@Override
public boolean commit() throws LoginException {
  // TODO Auto-generated method stub
  return true;
}

@Override
public boolean logout() throws LoginException {
  // TODO Auto-generated method stub
  return false;
}

public void initialize(Subject subject, CallbackHandler
  callbackHandler,
  Map<String, ?> state, Map<String, ?> options) {
  this.subject = subject;
  try {
    NameCallback nameCallback = new
    NameCallback("prompt");
    PasswordCallback passwordCallback = new
      PasswordCallback("prompt", false);
    callbackHandler.handle(new Callback[]{nameCallback,
      passwordCallback});
    password = new
      String(passwordCallback.getPassword());
    username = nameCallback.getName();
```

```
    } catch (Exception e) {
      throw new RuntimeException(e);
    }
  }
}
```

3. Configure Spring Security with JAAS.

```xml
<sec:authentication-manager>
  <sec:authentication-provider ref="jaasAuthProvider" />
</sec:authentication-manager>
<bean id="jaasAuthProvider" class="org.springframework.
  security.authentication.jaas.
  DefaultJaasAuthenticationProvider">
  <property name="configuration">
    <bean class="org.springframework.security.
      authentication.jaas.memory.InMemoryConfiguration">
      <constructor-arg>
        <map><entry key="SPRINGSECURITY">
          <array>
            <bean class="javax.security.auth.
              login.AppConfigurationEntry">
            <constructor-arg value="org.packt.
              springsecurityjaas.LoginModuleImpl" />
            <constructor-arg>
              <util:constant static-field="javax.
              security.auth.login.AppConfigurationEntry
                $LoginModuleControlFlag.REQUIRED" />
            </constructor-arg>
            <constructor-arg>
              <map></map>
            </constructor-arg>
          </bean>
        </array>
      </entry>
      </map>
    </constructor-arg>
  </bean>
</property>
<property name="authorityGranters">
  <list>
    <bean class="org.packt.springsecurityjaas.
      AuthorityGranterImpl" />
  </list>
</property>
</bean>
</beans>
```

How it works...

Access the URL: `http://localhost:8080/SpringSecurity_Jaas/`

Log in using the following credentials: `publisher/publisher123` and `editor/editor123`.

The authentication is handled by `DefaultJaasAuthenticationProvider`. The user information and authentication is handled by `InMemoryConfiguration`, which implies that the `LoginModule` class of JAAS does the authentication and authorization using `callbackhandlers`. On successful authentication, user is redirected to the authorized page. The following screenshots show the workflow of the application:

See also

▶ The *Spring Security with multiple authentication providers* recipe

▶ The *Spring Security with multiple input authentications* recipe

▶ The *Spring Security with JAAS* recipe

Index

logged in user info, obtaining 53-57

used, with digest-based Spring Security 43-45

used, with hashing-based Spring Security 43-45

Struts 2 application

ApacheDS, authenticating with 59-64

integrating, with Spring Security 41-43

T

Twitter

accessing with Spring Social, Spring Security used 226-228

U

UserDetailsService

used, for Spring Security with hibernate 210-213

V

Vaadin

URL 154

Vaadin form

using 165-173

W

Wicket

used, for Multitenancy 192-198

Wicket application

setting up 176, 177

Wicket authorization

Spring authentication, implementing with 187-191

Thank you for buying
Spring Security 3.x Cookbook

About Packt Publishing

Packt, pronounced 'packed', published its first book "*Mastering phpMyAdmin for Effective MySQL Management*" in April 2004 and subsequently continued to specialize in publishing highly focused books on specific technologies and solutions.

Our books and publications share the experiences of your fellow IT professionals in adapting and customizing today's systems, applications, and frameworks. Our solution based books give you the knowledge and power to customize the software and technologies you're using to get the job done. Packt books are more specific and less general than the IT books you have seen in the past. Our unique business model allows us to bring you more focused information, giving you more of what you need to know, and less of what you don't.

Packt is a modern, yet unique publishing company, which focuses on producing quality, cutting-edge books for communities of developers, administrators, and newbies alike. For more information, please visit our website: www.packtpub.com.

About Packt Open Source

In 2010, Packt launched two new brands, Packt Open Source and Packt Enterprise, in order to continue its focus on specialization. This book is part of the Packt Open Source brand, home to books published on software built around Open Source licences, and offering information to anybody from advanced developers to budding web designers. The Open Source brand also runs Packt's Open Source Royalty Scheme, by which Packt gives a royalty to each Open Source project about whose software a book is sold.

Writing for Packt

We welcome all inquiries from people who are interested in authoring. Book proposals should be sent to author@packtpub.com. If your book idea is still at an early stage and you would like to discuss it first before writing a formal book proposal, contact us; one of our commissioning editors will get in touch with you.

We're not just looking for published authors; if you have strong technical skills but no writing experience, our experienced editors can help you develop a writing career, or simply get some additional reward for your expertise.

Instant Spring Security Starter

ISBN: 978-1-78216-883-6   Paperback: 70 pages

Learn the fundamentals of web authentication and authorization using Spring Security

1. Learn something new in an Instant! A short, fast, focused guide delivering immediate results

2. Learn basic login/password and two-phase authentication

3. Secure access all the way from frontend to backend

4. Learn about the available security models, SPEL, and pragmatic considerations

Spring Security 3.1

ISBN: 978-1-84951-826-0   Paperback: 456 pages

Secure your applications from hackers with this step-by-step guide

1. Learn to leverage the power of Spring Security to keep intruders at bay through simple examples that illustrate real world problems

2. Each sample demonstrates key concepts allowing you to build your knowledge of the architecture in a practical and incremental way

3. Filled with samples that clearly illustrate how to integrate with the technologies and frameworks of your choice

Please check **www.PacktPub.com** for information on our titles

www.ingramcontent.com/pod-product-compliance
Lightning Source LLC
Chambersburg PA
CBHW060516060326
40690CB00017B/3305